ON THE WAY
to the
FUTURE

ON THE WAY
to the
FUTURE

DANIEL'S VISIONS
and the BELIEVER'S HOPE

RAY C. STEDMAN

With James D. Denney

DISCOVERY HOUSE
PUBLISHERS®

Feeding the Soul with the Word of God

Discovery House is affiliated with RBC Ministries,
Grand Rapids, Michigan.

Requests for permission to quote from this book should be directed to:
Permissions Department, Discovery House Publishers, P.O. Box 3566,
Grand Rapids, MI 49501, or contact us by e-mail at
permissionsdept@dhp.org

Library of Congress Cataloging-in-Publication Data

Stedman, Ray C.
    On the way to the future : Daniel's visions and the believer's
hope / Ray C. Stedman ; with James D. Denney.
        p.   cm.
    ISBN 978-1-57293-796-3
    1. Bible. Daniel—Prophecies. 2. Bible. Daniel—Criticism,
interpretation, etc. I. Title.
BS1556.S74 2013
224'.5015—dc23   2013036325

Printed in the United States of America
Second printing in 2014

CONTENTS

Publisher's Preface

From 1950 to 1990, Ray Stedman (1917–1992) served as pastor of the Peninsula Bible Church in Palo Alto, California. He was known and loved as a man of outstanding Bible knowledge, Christian integrity, warmth, and humility. Born in Temvik, North Dakota, Stedman grew up on the rugged landscape of Montana. When he was a small child, his mother became ill and his father, a railroad man, abandoned the family. Ray grew up on his aunt's Montana farm from the time he was six. He came to know the Lord at a Methodist revival meeting at age ten.

As a young man he moved around and tried different jobs, working in Chicago, Denver, Hawaii, and elsewhere. During World War II, he enlisted in the Navy, where he often led Bible studies for civilians and Navy personnel, and he even preached on local radio in Hawaii. At the close of the war, Stedman was married in Honolulu (he and his wife, Elaine, had first met in Great Falls, Montana). They returned to the mainland in 1946, and he graduated from Dallas Theological Seminary in 1950. After two summers interning under Dr. J. Vernon McGee, Stedman traveled for several months with Dr. H. A. Ironside, pastor of Moody Church in Chicago.

In 1950, Stedman was called by the two-year-old Peninsula Bible Fellowship to serve as its first pastor. Peninsula Bible Fellowship became Peninsula Bible Church, and Pastor Stedman served a forty-year tenure, retiring on April 30, 1990. During those years, he authored a number of life-changing Christian books, including the classic work on the meaning and mission of the church, *Body Life*. He went into the presence of his Lord on October 7, 1992.

On the Way to the Future is edited and updated from a sermon series Stedman preached in the late 1960s. Chapter 1 offers an overview of Daniel's life, including his ordeal in the lions' den; the story of his friends, Shadrach, Meshach, and Abednego in the fiery furnace; and the story of the handwriting on the wall. The rest of the book is devoted to the prophetic passages of the book of Daniel.

The amazing predictions in Daniel deal with events on earth just prior to the return of Jesus Christ to establish His kingdom. Although the events predicted in the book of Daniel could occur within our lifetime, we have to recognize that the times and the seasons belong to God alone. These predicted events might be delayed for many years or even centuries.

Bible prophecy does not give us an exact timetable of future events. Rather, it provides highlights of history, and it is often difficult to tell how much time elapses between predicted events. The purpose of Bible prophecy is not to increase our knowledge or satisfy our curiosity but to encourage us toward a life of deeper obedience, righteousness, and faith. The focus of all Bible prophecy is the King of Kings, Jesus the Lord, who is coming to put an end to sin, suffering, oppression, war, and death. That is the uplifting message of the book of Daniel for our lives.

—Discovery House Publishers

1

ON THE WAY TO THE FUTURE

Introduction and Overview

People are endlessly fascinated by Bible prophecy. The prophecies of Daniel and Revelation have been sensationalized into best-selling books and major motion pictures. They have been exploited and distorted in the headlines of supermarket tabloids. People want to know what the future holds—especially if the future is as bizarre and sensational as many books and films make it seem.

But Bible prophecy is serious business. God did not entrust visions of the future to such prophets as Daniel, Jeremiah, Ezekiel, and John merely to thrill and entertain us. God gave us the prophetic books of the Bible as a guide to His plan for history. Yes, the prophecies of Scripture were meant to inform us about the future—but more important, they were meant to instruct us for the present. God gave us these books so we would know how to live today with tomorrow in mind. He gave them to us to sober us and ground us in His eternal perspective on human and heavenly events.

The predictions contained in Daniel and Revelation have not yet been fulfilled in their entirety. These two books, one from the Old Testament and one from the New, remarkably complement each other in their symmetry and harmony. The book of Revelation explains the book of Daniel. The book of Daniel lays the basis for the book of Revelation. If you want to know God's program for the future, you must first understand the book of Daniel.

Knowledge of the future can be both dangerous and wonderful. Imagine what would happen if you possessed the ability to know what would happen tomorrow or next week. Think of the advantage it would give you in the stock market, in buying insurance, and in other practical matters of life.

Then again, think of the anguish you would feel if you knew that an unavoidable loss or calamity was headed your way. Jesus had good reason for saying, "Do not worry about tomorrow, for tomorrow will worry about itself. Each day has enough trouble of its own" (Matthew 6:34).

God does not unfold the future to us in specific detail. He does not disclose your individual future or mine. What He does show us in the prophetic books of the Bible is the general trend of events, the outline of His program, and the way His plan for history is certain to end. Anyone who investigates prophecy in a careful, objective way will find helpful information about both future and present events. All events in the world are carrying out God's purpose on earth. These events will unfold exactly as He has foretold them. We can understand the present only in the light of God's prophetic agenda.

In the book of Daniel, as in the book of Revelation, God clothes the prophetic passages in symbolic language. He presents them to us in figurative form. That's why we see such strange and frightening images—startling signs in nature, strange beasts with many different heads and horns, glimpses of shattering worldwide events, and more. These prophetic symbols have always puzzled readers of Daniel.

THE TWO LEVELS OF THE BOOK OF DANIEL

The book of Daniel is actually written on two levels. First, there is the drama of Daniel and his three Hebrew friends: Hananiah,

Mishael, and Azariah. We see them living exemplary lives of wisdom, faith, and courage during a time of extreme danger, oppression, and political upheaval. They have been uprooted from their homeland of Judah and now live as exiles in Babylon. During the course of this narrative, they find themselves serving, first, Nebuchadnezzar, the king of Babylon, and later, the Persian conquerors of Babylon. It's a thrilling narrative filled with heroism, suspense, and intrigue. That is the first level of the book of Daniel.

Woven into this historical narrative is a prophetic account of future events, couched in symbolic images. That is the second level of the book of Daniel. You can't read the prophetic portion of Daniel as if it were a novel. To study Daniel's prophecies, you must take the entire length and breadth of the Bible into account as you interpret its symbols. The vivid symbolism contained in the book of Daniel serve as a "padlock" God has placed on the book to keep curious sensation-seekers from unlocking the holy secrets of God's agenda.

A second "padlock" God has placed on the prophecies of Daniel is the fact that God places six chapters of narrative history and moral teaching in the book before the prophetic section. God wants to lead us into an understanding of the moral character He requires of us before He introduces His prophetic program. The prophecies make no sense without the practical, moral instruction God presents to us in the lives of Daniel and his three friends. To understand what the prophetic program means, you must first grasp the moral lessons of the first six chapters of the book. There are no shortcuts to wisdom.

God's prophetic books were not given to us as an intellectual puzzle to be solved but as profound truth to be integrated into our daily experience. That's the beauty of God's Word: It can't be understood by the intellect alone. It must be understood by the entire being, including the soul and spirit. Many people are content to sit down with prophetic outlines of Daniel and Revelation, to draw charts of future history, and to analyze eschatology and doctrine down to a gnat's eyebrow. But until you incorporate the spiritual lessons of Daniel into your life, you will not experience the true blessing that flows from this amazing Old Testament book.

Many of the great truths of the New Testament are built upon the foundation of Old Testament truth found in the book of Daniel. The Lord Jesus himself made this clear during the Olivet Discourse after His disciples asked Him what the symbol of His return to earth would be. Jesus said, "So when you see standing in the holy place 'the abomination that causes desolation,' spoken of through the prophet Daniel—let the reader understand—then let those who are in Judea flee to the mountains" (Matthew 24:15–16).

When Matthew adds, "let the reader understand," he means, "Don't read the prophetic passages carelessly or superficially. You have to grasp the full import of Scripture to recognize the abomination of desolation when it comes." The world, in its superficial approach to truth, will not recognize that day when it comes. People will cry, "Peace, peace!" when there is no peace, and destruction will come upon them. They will be swept away just as the people of Noah's day were swept away by the flood. Jesus does not want us to be destroyed through ignorance, so He encourages us to seek a practical, applied, experiential understanding of the prophetic truths of Scripture.

THE STRUCTURE OF DANIEL

The book of Daniel divides into two sections. The first six chapters, which are devoted to moral and spiritual instruction, present the history and drama of the prophet Daniel himself and his friends in the land of Babylon. Here is an outline of the book of Daniel:

THE LIFE OF DANIEL IN BABYLON (Daniel 1–6)

1. Daniel interprets Nebuchadnezzar's dream of the great image (2)
2. Nebuchadnezzar's image of gold (3)
3. Daniel interprets Nebuchadnezzar's vision of a great tree (4)

The book of Daniel contains a story of faith lived out in the fiery crucible of a hostile world. The vivid example of Daniel and his companions becomes increasingly more relevant to our lives as we realize that we are living in post-Christian times, in an increasingly hostile and anti-Christian world.

If you find yourself struggling to live the Christian life amid the pressures, temptations, and persecution of this secular age, then the first six chapters of Daniel are a must-read for you. If you work in an office surrounded by godless coworkers who continually take the Lord's name in vain; if your employer pressures you to commit unethical acts on the job; if your friends challenge you to compromise your faith or your morality; or if the law of the land says you cannot be a witness for Christ—then the first six chapters of Daniel will guide you, comfort you, and instruct you.

These chapters are especially valuable and inspiring for young Christians who must stand against peer pressure and temptation, because these chapters record the actions of a group of teenagers who were taken captive by King Nebuchadnezzar and carried off from Judah to the pagan land of Babylon.

As these godly young men began their career of faith, they did so with all the insecurities that are normal for young people in a hostile culture. Daniel and his teenage friends had to take a stand against false religion, social pressure, and persecution, much as young Christians today are called to stand firm against occultism, paganism, illicit sex, and substance abuse. It was a matter of life and death in Daniel's time—and the stakes are just as high today. So Daniel and his friends are encouraging, instructive role models for today's Christian youth.

STANDING FIRM UNDER PRESSURE AND TEMPTATION

The story opens during the reign of wicked King Jehoiakim of Judah, a vassal king who was installed by Pharaoh Necho II of Egypt. Jehoiakim paid a rich tribute of silver and gold to Egypt, which he raised through heavy taxes on the people of Judah (see 2 Kings 23:35). After the Egyptians were defeated in battle by the Babylonians, Jehoiakim switched allegiances and paid tribute to the Babylonians—but he later switched his allegiance back to Egypt, angering Babylon's King Nebuchadnezzar II.

In 599 BC, Nebuchadnezzar sent his armies into Judah, laid siege to Jerusalem, and conquered the city. Daniel 1:2 tells us that "the Lord delivered Jehoiakim king of Judah into his [Nebuchadnezzar's] hand, along with some of the articles from the temple of God. These he carried off to the temple of his god in Babylonia and put in the treasure house of his god."

Nebuchadnezzar also ordered the chief of his court officials to take some of the leading young men of Jerusalem's royal family and nobility into custody and bring them to Babylon to serve the king. These young men should be "without any physical defect, handsome, showing aptitude for every kind of learning, well informed, quick to understand, and qualified to serve in the king's palace," and they would be taught "the language and literature of the Babylonians"

(Daniel 1:4). After three years of intensive training, they would serve in Nebuchadnezzar's court.

As the book opens, four of these exiled young Hebrews—Daniel, Hananiah, Mishael, and Azariah (who have been renamed Belteshazzar, Shadrach, Meshach, and Abednego by their Babylonian captors)—are pressured to change their diet. Ordinarily, diet would not be a particularly significant issue, but God had already instructed these young men as to what they could and could not eat. The foods God had told them not to eat were the very foods the Babylonians *required* them to eat as prisoners and servants of the king of Babylon.

What could these young men do? King Nebuchadnezzar was an immensely powerful and merciless tyrant. Later in his book, Daniel describes Nebuchadnezzar as a king of near matchless "sovereignty and greatness and glory and splendor. Because of the high position he [God] gave him, all the nations and peoples of every language dreaded and feared him. Those the king wanted to put to death, he put to death; those he wanted to spare, he spared; those he wanted to promote, he promoted; and those he wanted to humble, he humbled" (Daniel 5:18–19). Few human leaders, before or since, ever wielded as much authority as King Nebuchadnezzar.

The cruelty of King Nebuchadnezzar was unparalleled. On one occasion, he laid siege to Jerusalem, causing Judah's King Zedekiah to flee with his army. When Nebuchadnezzar's forces captured Zedekiah, he demonstrated his cruelty by executing the sons of Zedekiah before his eyes, then putting out Zedekiah's eyes so that this horror would be the last thing the grieving king would ever see. Then Zedekiah was led in chains to a life of slavery in Babylon (see 2 Kings 25:1–7). Nebuchadnezzar also had two false prophets roasted slowly to death over a fire (see Jeremiah 29:21–22). This king was an expert in torture, and his word was law.

So Daniel, Hananiah, Mishael, and Azariah faced an extreme moral test, knowing they had to comply with the king's demands or risk death by torture. What could they do? Under such pressure, should they heed the advice, "When in Rome, do as the Romans do"? It's the same argument people often use today: "Everybody else is doing it." Would it really be so wrong to eat a ham sandwich with the Babylonians—especially if that sandwich would save you from torture and death? Who would know or care?

Yet these four young Hebrews, at the risk of life itself, chose to stand firmly for their principles and their God. And God gave them the grace to maintain their righteous stand in spite of pressure and threats. Daniel asked that he and his friends be given nothing but vegetables to eat, and after ten days these young men looked healthier than those who ate the royal meat.

As a result, Daniel and his friends were exalted and were given positions of responsibility in the land of their captivity. The king found their wisdom and advice to be wiser and more reliable than that of the Babylonian wise men and enchanters. This turn of events reminds us of how God exalted Joseph in Egypt when he maintained his integrity before God.

As we will see, however, the pressure did not end for these young men of Judah. It continued and intensified in the chapters that followed.

A TROUBLING DREAM

Daniel 2 reveals why God allowed these young men to come under intense testing. One night, King Nebuchadnezzar dreamed about a great image of a man with a strange body. The image had a head of gold, shoulders of silver, a midsection of bronze, legs of iron, and feet of mixed clay and iron. The next morning, the king called in the Babylonian wise men and ordered them to tell him not only the interpretation of the dream but also the actual details of the dream. He expected these magicians to describe what had transpired within the king's sleeping brain—and if they failed, they would be executed.

You have to give the king credit. He had devised a brilliant test for his astrologers and sorcerers. They claimed to possess the supernatural power to discern mysteries and secrets. Well, if they truly had such power, then they should be able to describe the king's dream as well as interpret it. If they couldn't describe the dream, then they must be frauds. The king's wise men could not describe the king's dream, so they were condemned to death.

The king had not asked Daniel to interpret his dream. But because he was considered one of the king's wise men, he was under the execution order as well. When Daniel asked the captain of the king's guard why he and the others were to be executed, the captain explained the situation. So Daniel pleaded for the lives of the other wise men and asked to be brought before the king to reveal and interpret the dream.

The night before Daniel was to appear before the king, he and his three Hebrew friends prayed together, asking God for mercy and for an answer to the king's question. Later that night, God revealed the king's dream to Daniel in a vision.

The next day, Daniel appeared before the king, revealed the dream, and interpreted it—and Daniel humbly gave all glory to God. "No wise man, enchanter, magician or diviner can explain to the king the mystery he has asked about," Daniel explained, "but there is a God in heaven who reveals mysteries. He has shown King Nebuchadnezzar what will happen in days to come" (see Daniel 2:27–28).

The head of gold in Nebuchadnezzar's dream symbolized the Babylonian kingdom; the shoulders of silver symbolized Medo-Persia; the midsection of bronze represented the coming empire of Greece; the two legs of iron represented the two divisions of the Roman Empire; and feet of mingled iron and clay represented the disunited, part-strong, part-weak remnant of the broken Roman Empire. This great prophetic passage outlines history from Daniel's day to a future that is still beyond our own day.

As the prophet watched Nebuchadnezzar's dream, he saw a stone that had not been cut by a human hand. The stone struck the feet of the image and utterly demolished it from head to toe. The fragments blew away on the wind like chaff, but the stone grew to become a great mountain that filled the entire earth (see Daniel 2:34–35). This event symbolized a time when the last kingdom would be shattered by a divine agency (not of human hands). As we shall later see, that stone represents Jesus himself, and that stone will usher in the worldwide kingdom of God and the reign of Jesus Christ.

When King Nebuchadnezzar heard Daniel describe and interpret his dream, he fell on his face before Daniel and honored the prophet and his God. "Surely your God is the God of gods and the Lord of kings," said King Nebuchadnezzar, "and a revealer of mysteries, for you were able to reveal this mystery" (see Daniel 2:47).

God's servant Daniel proved he was willing to stand and obey God despite the threat of torture and death. God delivered Daniel because this faithful young man trusted in the invisible God who rules human affairs. That's one of the key lessons of the book of Daniel. As the young prophet said in his grateful prayer to God:

> "Praise be to the name of God for ever and ever;
>   wisdom and power are his.
> He changes times and seasons;
>   he deposes kings and raises up others.
> He gives wisdom to the wise
>   and knowledge to the discerning.
> He reveals deep and hidden things;
>   he knows what lies in darkness,
>   and light dwells with him." (Daniel 2:20–22)

If you live in bold obedience to the living God of the universe, you need not fear the wrath of kings. The same God who created the world is able to work out every circumstance of your life, no matter how impossible it may seem. We will see this theme repeated five times during the first six chapters of the book of Daniel.

You and I live in a situation not unlike that faced by Daniel. The prevailing "wisdom" of this world states that there is no God—or, if He does exist, He has no power and is not actively involved in the world. According to worldly "wisdom," God doesn't affect history and

He doesn't affect human lives. God makes no difference in the world. That's the philosophy most opinion leaders in our world have adopted.

But if you walk faithfully, if you obey what God says regardless of pressure or threats, God will place you in a strategic position and use you in a mighty way. He will give you the privilege of opening the eyes of men and women to the fact that God exists, that He is active and involved in human events, and that *He must be reckoned with*. That is the message of the book of Daniel.

TESTED BY FIRE

Daniel 3 relates the story of the fiery furnace. Daniel's three Hebrew companions, Shadrach, Meshach, and Abednego, were commanded to bow down before an image King Nebuchadnezzar had erected in his own honor. If the Statue of Liberty were to lower her torch, she would be about 20 feet taller, from feet to crown, than the image of Nebuchadnezzar on the Babylonian plain.

The king gathered the crowd, including Shadrach, Meshach, and Abednego, on the plain. All the people were commanded to bow down and worship the image—and the command was punctuated by the stoking of a great sacrificial furnace erected at the other end of the plain. All who refused to bow to the image would die in the furnace. A band played a variety of instruments—horn, flute, zither, lyre, harp, and pipes—as a call to worship. At the sound of the first musical chord, all the people fell prostrate and worshiped the king's image—

All except Shadrach, Meshach, and Abednego. When these three young Hebrew men were brought before Nebuchadnezzar for their refusal to bow, he gave them one last chance, ordering them to fall down and worship. They respectfully declined, saying:

> "King Nebuchadnezzar, we do not need to defend ourselves before you in this matter. If we are thrown into the blazing furnace, the God we serve is able to deliver

us from it, and he will deliver us from Your Majesty's hand. But even if he does not, we want you to know, Your Majesty, that we will not serve your gods or worship the image of gold you have set up." (Daniel 3:16–18)

Even though these three men expected God to rescue them, they trusted God no matter what their fate—even if God would not deliver them from the fire. They placed obedience to God above life itself. Even a horrible death in the flames of the furnace could not dissuade or intimidate them. So God honored them in a mighty way, taking them safely through the furnace.

The king sent Shadrach, Meshach, and Abednego into the furnace, and the fire was so hot that the soldiers who threw them in were killed. But when King Nebuchadnezzar looked into the furnace, he saw four men walking in the furnace, completely unharmed—and the fourth, the king said, looked "like a son of the gods" (3:25). When the king called the Hebrews out of the furnace, they emerged safe and whole, without even the scent of fire on them (v. 27).

Once again King Nebuchadnezzar was moved to worship God: "Praise be to the God of Shadrach, Meshach and Abednego, who has sent his angel and rescued his servants! They trusted in him and defied the king's command and were willing to give up their lives rather than serve or worship any god except their own God. Therefore I decree that the people of any nation or language who say anything against the God of Shadrach, Meshach and Abednego be cut into pieces and their houses be turned into piles of rubble, for no other god can save in this way" (Daniel 3:28–29).

And the king promoted Shadrach, Meshach and Abednego to positions of even greater responsibility in the kingdom of Babylon.

THE TESTIMONY OF THE KING

In Daniel 4, we witness the conversion of Nebuchadnezzar. Again the king dreams and again Daniel reveals and interprets the dream. The message of the dream is that the king will descend into insanity, will eat grass like cattle, and will live with the wild animals—but his kingdom will be returned to him when he acknowledges God, renounces sin, and shows kindness to the oppressed.

In accordance with Daniel's prophecy, the king went mad for seven years, eating grass in the field with the animals, though his throne was preserved throughout this time. Why did God use this particular means of getting the king's attention? God did so because He wanted to show what happens to human beings who reject fellowship with the living God: They become beastly and brutish.

When the king's reason was restored to him by the grace of God, Nebuchadnezzar issued a statement of faith—his testimony of how God had humbled him, allowed him to tumble into madness, then brought him back to sanity. Nebuchadnezzar concluded, "Now I, Nebuchadnezzar, praise and exalt and glorify the King of heaven, because everything he does is right and all his ways are just. And those who walk in pride he is able to humble" (Daniel 4:37).

Who restored King Nebuchadnezzar to sanity? The same One who took away his sanity: Almighty God. Our sovereign God chose to use Daniel and his friends to capture the heart of the greatest king of the greatest empire of the ancient world. This same God is pleased to use you and me to capture hearts for His kingdom in our own day.

THE HANDWRITING ON THE WALL

Daniel 5 presents the familiar story of King Belshazzar and the handwriting on the wall. As the story opens, we see the luxury and immorality of the kingdom of Babylon. King Nebuchadnezzar disappears from Daniel's narrative without explanation, but history records that his reign ended in 562 BC. Nebuchadnezzar was succeeded by several kings who are not mentioned in the book of Daniel.

Nebuchadnezzar's immediate successor was Amel-Marduk, who reigned for a mere two years. The ancient historian Berossus tells us he was murdered by agents of his brother-in-law, Nergal-Sharezer, who then took the throne. Nergal-Sharezer was mentioned in Jeremiah 39:13 as a high official in Nebuchadnezzar's court. He reigned from 560 to 556 BC, and was followed by his son Labashi-Marduk, who ruled for less than a year before being murdered in a palace coup. Labashi-Marduk's successor, King Nabonidus, reigned over Babylon from 556 to 539 BC.

History records that during his reign King Nabonidus began to lose interest in governing the nation, and he became more and more involved in the Babylonian religion. Nabonidus would spend months at the temple of Sîn, the Babylonian moon god (his mother was a priestess there). When King Nabonidus was away from the palace in Babylon, he left his son, Belshazzar, in command. As we come to Daniel 5, we find that Daniel has skipped over all of this Babylonian history, because the palace intrigues of pagan kings are of little importance in God's view of history.

In Daniel 5, Nebuchadnezzar has exited the stage of history, and in his place we find Belshazzar, the drunkard son of an absent and uninvolved King Nabonidus. Daniel has served in the royal court through a steady procession of Babylonian kings, and he is still the prime minister of the kingdom. The self-centered and pleasure-seeking Belshazzar throws a party—a festival of debauchery and sin. Belshazzar, along with his wives, concubines, and guests, defile the gold and silver chalices that were taken from the temple in Jerusalem. The revelers drink wine from those sacred utensils and use them to toast their false gods.

In the midst of the party, a shocking supernatural event occurs: A disembodied human hand appears and its fingers write an inscription on the plaster of the wall—*Mene, Mene, Tekel, Parsin*. Belshazzar and his guests don't understand the inscription, but they are frightened by the apparition of the hand. Belshazzar calls for his magicians and astrologers to decipher the handwriting on the wall, and Daniel is brought before him. Daniel interprets the inscription as a judgment on Belshazzar for his arrogance:

> "Here is what these words mean:
>
> > *Mene*: God has numbered the days of your reign
> > and brought it to an end.
> > *Tekel*: You have been weighed on the scales and
> > found wanting.
> > *Parsin*: Your kingdom is divided and given to the
> > Medes and Persians."
>
> (Daniel 5:26–28)

The inscription *Mene, Mene, Tekel, Parsin* was unknown to the Babylonians because it was in Aramaic, a language similar to Hebrew. *Mene* comes from a root word meaning "to count," so Daniel told Belshazzar that God had counted or numbered the days of his kingdom and had brought it to an end. *Tekel* is an alternate spelling of *shekel*, a Jewish coin. The word means "to weigh." So Daniel told Belshazzar that he had been weighed on the moral and spiritual scales and was found to be lacking. *Parsin* is an apparent play on words. *Parsin* is a form of *peres*, which means "to divide." *Peres* also resembles the ancient word for Persia. So Daniel told Belshazzar, "Your kingdom is divided and given to the Medes and Persians."

That night, God's judgment was carried out against Belshazzar. He was killed, Babylon was conquered, and Darius the Mede became the ruler of Babylon. Daniel 5 illustrates the overarching theme of the book of Daniel: God is at work in human affairs and human history. Those who oppose God will ultimately be cast down. But those (like Daniel and his friends) who look beyond this visible realm to serve the invisible but mighty and sovereign God of heaven will receive all the power they need for true success.

DANIEL AND THE LIONS

In Daniel 6, we witness yet another demonstration of God's provision in seemingly hopeless circumstances. This chapter tells of Daniel's ordeal in the lions' den. At this time, Babylon is ruled by Darius the Mede. It's not clear if *Darius* is the king's name or his title, since *Darius* is an English transliteration of a Persian word that means "rich and kingly." Some Bible scholars think that Darius the Mede in the book of Daniel refers to Cyrus the Great (Cyrus II of Persia) or Darius the Great (Darius I, the third king of the Persian Achaemenid Empire).

King Darius was very fond of his advisor and prime minister, Daniel. But Daniel had jealous rivals. In an effort to destroy Daniel, these rivals maneuvered King Darius into issuing a decree forbidding anyone to pray to any god or king except Darius. They knew it was a decree that Daniel would not obey. In fact, Daniel clearly went out of his way to be "caught" praying, because he prayed three times daily at an open upstairs window where he would be seen by many. His enemies eagerly reported Daniel's "crime" to the king.

When these accusations were brought to King Darius, he looked for a loophole to excuse Daniel. But Daniel's enemies slyly reminded the king that, according to the law of the Medes and Persians, the king's decree could not be changed or revoked. So the king reluctantly sent Daniel to the lions' den with these words: "May your God, whom you serve continually, rescue you!" (Daniel 6:16). Daniel was sealed up in the den with the lions, and the king spent the night unable to eat or sleep. At dawn, the king got up, went to the den, and called to Daniel—and Daniel answered!

"May the king live forever!" the prophet replied. "My God sent his angel, and he shut the mouths of the lions. They have not hurt me, because I was found innocent in his sight. Nor have I ever done any wrong before you, Your Majesty" (Daniel 6:21–22). So Daniel was released, and the king ordered Daniel's rivals to be thrown to the lions instead. Then King Darius issued another decree in which he glorified Daniel's God as the one true God.

THE PROPHETIC SECTION BEGINS

The future-focused section of Daniel begins in chapter 7 with the vision of the four beasts. These four beasts cover the same period of time as the gold, silver, bronze, and iron divisions of the image Nebuchadnezzar saw in his dream in Daniel 2. The four beasts represent the same kingdoms—but from God's point of view instead of man's point of view. These kingdoms are not mighty powers in God's sight. They are merely beasts that growl and quarrel with each other. Daniel sees these nations struggling against each other, and their struggle culminates in the powerful reign of a single individual over the entire Western world.

In chapter 8 we see the movement of Western history. The ram and the he-goat come together in battle—a picture, as we are later told in chapter 11, of Alexander the Great's conquest and the rise of the Seleucid kingdom in Syria in opposition to the Ptolemies in Egypt. These two kingdoms occupied the center stage of history for centuries after the time of Daniel—a mighty struggle between Syria and Egypt, with little Israel caught in the middle. The battle raged back and forth, and even today Israel continues to be the most fought-over piece of real estate in the world. More battles have occurred in the land of Israel than in any other spot on the face of the earth, and the last great battle, Armageddon, will be fought in this region.

In the midst of this prophecy in chapter 9, Daniel pours his heart out to God in prayer. The answer to his prayer, in the last section of the chapter, is one of the most remarkable prophecies in the Bible. It is the prophecy of the seventy weeks. This is the timetable of prophecy concerning the nation of Israel. It gives us a principle that has been called "the Great Parenthesis"—an interpretation of Scripture suggesting that God has interrupted His program for Israel and has inserted this present age in which we live between the first coming and the second coming of the Lord Jesus.

This indeterminate period, which has now spanned some two thousand years, comes between the sixty-ninth week of years and the seventieth week of Daniel's prophecy. The seventieth week, a week of seven years, is yet to be fulfilled for Israel. This week of seven years is what the book of Revelation and other prophetic passages call "the great tribulation," the time of Jacob's trouble. It has been broken off from the other sixty-nine weeks, and it remains to be fulfilled.

THE INVISIBLE REALITY

Daniel 10 shines a light on the invisible reality that lies beyond this visible world. This is another great revelation of God's sovereign government in the affairs of humanity—and it is the explanation for the events of history. What causes the upheaval and strife in our world today? Clearly, there are unseen forces at work, and these forces are starkly revealed to Daniel in this passage.

As Daniel 10 opens, the prophet Daniel has gathered some of his friends together beside the Tigris River for a prayer meeting. He wants to learn God's will and stir up his people to return to Israel. As Daniel prays, something amazing happens:

> On the twenty-fourth day of the first month, as I was standing on the bank of the great river, the Tigris, I looked up and there before me was a man dressed in linen, with a belt of fine gold from Uphaz around his waist. His body was like topaz, his face like lightning, his eyes like flaming torches, his arms and legs like the gleam of burnished bronze, and his voice like the sound of a multitude. (Daniel 10:4–6)

Who is this amazing figure? We are reminded of the vision the apostle John had on the island of Patmos at the beginning of the book of Revelation:

> And among the lampstands was someone like a son of man, dressed in a robe reaching down to his feet and with

a golden sash around his chest. The hair on his head was white like wool, as white as snow, and his eyes were like blazing fire. His feet were like bronze glowing in a furnace, and his voice was like the sound of rushing waters. In his right hand he held seven stars, and coming out of his mouth was a sharp, double-edged sword. His face was like the sun shining in all its brilliance. (Revelation 1:13–16)

To Daniel by the Tigris River and to John on the island of Patmos, a curtain opened—the curtain that had separated our visible world from the invisible spiritual kingdom with its unseen warfare. Daniel and John were able to see the One to whom they had been praying moments before. That Person was there all the time. He had not suddenly appeared out of nowhere. But He was invisible until the curtain opened and their eyes could see. I believe it is unquestionably the Lord Jesus Christ who is revealed in both Daniel 10 and Revelation 1.

The prophet Daniel is being prepared to learn something remarkable from the man clothed in linen—a lesson in the mystery of prayer. The man says:

"Do not be afraid, Daniel. Since the first day that you set your mind to gain understanding and to humble yourself before your God, your words were heard, and I have come in response to them. But the prince of the Persian kingdom resisted me twenty-one days. Then Michael, one of the chief princes, came to help me, because I was detained there with the king of Persia. Now I have come to explain to you what will happen to your people in the future, for the vision concerns a time yet to come." (Daniel 10:12–14)

A second being now appears, an angel sent to help Daniel, described only as "one who looked like a man" (v. 18). The rest of the vision indicates that this is an angel sent from this great Person to help Daniel. He touches Daniel and helps him to his feet. The New Testament tells us that angels are "ministering spirits, sent forth to minister for them who shall be heirs of salvation" (Hebrews 1:14 KJV). They bring aid to God's people and help to carry out God's will on earth.

I once heard of a story from *Reader's Digest* about a soldier in the Vietnam War whose life was saved when an enemy bullet was stopped by a copy of the New Testament and Psalms he carried in his pocket. The bullet passed right through the four gospels, Acts, the epistles, and Revelation, finally coming to rest at the 91st Psalm—the passage that promises:

> You will not fear the terror of night,
>   nor the arrow that flies by day . . .
> For he will command his angels concerning you
>   to guard you in all your ways. (Psalm 91:5, 11)

That was no accident. That was the intervention of an angel. The invisible ministry of angels occurs continually, though we are largely unaware of their activity in our lives.

Daniel 10:2 tells us that Daniel spent three weeks fasting and praying—then the angel came to Daniel and said, "Do not be afraid, Daniel. Since the first day that you set your mind to gain understanding and to humble yourself before your God, your words were heard, and I have come in response to them. But the prince of the Persian kingdom resisted me twenty-one days" (Daniel 10:12–13). In other words, God heard Daniel's prayer on the very first day and sent an answer—but the answer Daniel sought was delayed while the angel battled the demon-prince of Persia for three weeks.

The lesson here is that when we pray, God's answer is on its way the moment we begin to ask. The answer may not arrive instantly, because God is working out all the circumstances that must be altered in order for that prayer to be answered. But God answers prayer immediately.

Prayer is not (as we tend to think) the means of getting God to do our bidding. Rather, prayer is the means by which we enlist ourselves in the thrilling activity of God and His angels in carrying out His agenda for the world. God eagerly desires our involvement in His eternal plan. He wants us to ask Him to do what He says He will do—and He often will not do it *unless* we ask Him. That's why James says, "You do not have because you do not ask" (James 4:2). If you ask, God will do what He has promised.

Although God's answer to prayer is immediate, delays are possible. Why? In part, it's because we live in a fallen world, infested with fallen spirits—demons—who oppose God's work. Some of these evil spirits are related to the nations of the earth, such as the evil spirit referred to here as "the prince of the Persian kingdom" (Daniel 10:13). Once we understand that the events we read about in the newspapers are being stirred by warring angels behind the scenes of history, the frightening events in the world—from riots to terrorism to wars between nations—become easier to understand.

As Paul tells us, "For our struggle is not against flesh and blood, but against the rulers, against the authorities, against the powers of this dark world and against the spiritual forces of evil in the heavenly realms" (Ephesians 6:12). That's what the man clothed in linen and the angel tell Daniel: Behind the affairs of earth is an invisible hierarchy of evil, which has authority over kingdoms. Without doubt, there are evil angels that have authority over the nations of our world today, stirring up trouble, seeking to thwart God's eternal plan.

Chapter 11 is one of the most remarkable chapters in the Bible. It records a prophecy that, in one sense, has already been fulfilled in detail. It tells of the struggle between the king of Syria ("the king of the North") and the king of Egypt ("the king of the South") that took place after Daniel's time. These two kingdoms fought back and forth over the course of about one hundred thirty years. Israel, caught between the two warring nations, became a battlefield. Jerusalem was captured and sacked by both sides throughout the conflict. To live in Jerusalem in those days was to be like wheat being ground between two millstones.

As previously noted, this detailed prophecy was confirmed in detail by historical events—in one sense. Yet there is another sense in which this prophecy will be fulfilled again in the future. Like many prophetic passages of the Bible, Daniel 11 is subject to a double interpretation and a double fulfillment. We will explore this second fulfillment later in this book.

THE SEVENTIETH WEEK

We come to an interesting break where the angel says to Daniel:

> "Some of the wise will stumble, so that they may be refined, purified and made spotless until the time of the end, for it will still come at the appointed time.
>
> "The king will do as he pleases. He will exalt and magnify himself above every god and will say unheard-of things against the God of gods. He will be successful until the time of wrath is completed, for what has been determined must take place." (Daniel 11:35–36)

Here we begin the discussion of the seventieth week of Daniel, the tribulation period that is yet to be fulfilled—the last days, just before the return of Jesus Christ. This passage predicts an invasion of Palestine and a counterinvasion from Egypt in the south, and then there will be a meeting of two great armies in the land of Israel and the ultimate destruction of those armies on the plain between the Mediterranean Sea and the mountains of Israel. This event is described in various prophetic passages of Scripture, including Ezekiel 38–39 and Joel 2.

The beginning of Daniel 12 introduces the culminating event of all human history: the second coming of Christ. This event is accompanied by the resurrection of the dead:

"Multitudes who sleep in the dust of the earth will awake: some to everlasting life, others to shame and everlasting contempt." (Daniel 12:2)

In this final section, Daniel 12, the prophet Daniel asks questions of the man clothed in linen. The man (who is the preincarnate Christ) permits Daniel to understand two great forces at work in the world: good and evil. Some people want to believe that humanity is making progress, that education is advancing, that technology is making life better and better. Others make an even more convincing case that advancing technology only gives us more advanced ways to kill ourselves, to take away our privacy and freedom, to complicate our lives and strip away our humanity.

The book of Daniel makes it clear that we will never understand what is happening in the world until we accept the reality of the contest between good and evil. We need to realize that evil forces are at war against God behind the scenes of history. As the man clothed in linen tells Daniel:

"Go your way, Daniel, because the words are rolled up and sealed until the time of the end. Many will be purified, made spotless and refined, but the wicked will continue to be wicked. None of the wicked will understand, but those who are wise will understand." (Daniel 12:9–10)

Today, evil is more widespread than it has ever been. Our current era—with two world wars, genocidal assaults on humanity, the spread of terrorism, and the proliferation of weapons of mass destruction—is the most murderous, blood-drenched era in human history. The evil of our age is widespread and Satan inspired.

Against this backdrop, the righteousness of God contrasts sharply with the evil of this age. These two contrasting forces, good and evil, are at war in human society. Neither shall overpower the other until the end of the age. Good and evil are headed for a final conflict. At that precise moment in history, God will directly intervene in human affairs. There will be a final clash between these two principles. Of that conflict, the man clothed in linen says:

> "From the time that the daily sacrifice is abolished and the abomination that causes desolation is set up, there will be 1,290 days. Blessed is the one who waits for and reaches the end of the 1,335 days.
>
> "As for you, go your way till the end. You will rest, and then at the end of the days you will rise to receive your allotted inheritance." (Daniel 12:11–13)

Every nation and individual serves God. Some serve Him willingly—and some unwillingly. Even if a king renounces God ten times over, our God is sovereign. His eternal plan cannot fail. He works all events, all human choices, and all satanic chaos into His purposes. Nebuchadnezzar, Darius, Alexander, Caesar, Herod, Caiaphas, Pontius Pilate, Stalin, Hitler, Mao, Saddam, Osama bin Laden—none of these people could resist the will of God. None could hinder His agenda. The purposes of God roll irresistibly through time and space, encompassing billions of lives, including yours and mine.

The choice you and I must make is the choice between being willing tools in God's hands—or unwilling. We choose whether to receive the blessings of obedience—or the judgment that accompanies rebellion. The good news of Daniel is that God is alive and at work in the affairs of people and nations. Lions cannot consume us, the fiery furnace cannot scorch us, and tyrants cannot separate us from the love of King Jesus.

As we continue our journey through the events in this prophecy, let us step boldly and courageously with absolute confidence in our sovereign God.

2

WHEN DREAMS COME TRUE

Daniel 2:19–45

The world God created for us to live on is a beautiful planet—a place of natural scenic wonders, from the frosted heights of the Himalayas to the multicolored depths of the Grand Canyon. It teems with millions of species of plant and animal life. The vision of the sun's rays breaking through the clouds in a glorious sunset reminds us of the glory and majesty of our Creator.

But there is another world on planet earth—the human world, the fallen world, the world of human sin and strife. It's the world of insanity, anxiety, despair, suicide, abuse, and dysfunctional families. It's the world of wars, terrorism, and the threat of annihilation by nuclear or biological warfare. It's the world of recession, depression, and runaway inflation.

Even in this Internet age, this era of instant gratification and endless entertainment, we see generations of young people without hope, believing they have no future. They find no sense or meaning in life. They amuse themselves and while away the time until their world comes to an end through an ecological catastrophe, economic collapse, the population bomb, terrorism, global war, or some other form of Armageddon.

Decades ago, during the earliest years of the computer age, I had a conversation with Dr. Gerhard Dirks, a scientist who invented many of the most important computer memory systems. He said that there are three instruments of our society that have inflicted widespread despair on our culture: television, the computer, and the nuclear bomb.

Television brings all the horrors of our fallen world flooding into our living rooms, filling us with conscious fear and subliminal anxiety. The computer has depersonalized our lives—stripping away our privacy and turning us into mouse-clicking zombies. Even in our post-Cold-War age, we know that nuclear weapons still threaten us with annihilation. Once possessed only by great superpowers, these bombs could show up in the hands of stateless terrorists at any time. This disquieting knowledge produces despair and desperation in many lives today.

In view of the darkness and uncertainty of this world, I am all the more impressed by Peter's characterization of biblical prophecy as "something completely reliable" and "a light shining in a dark place." In his second epistle, Peter wrote about prophetic books of the Bible, such as the book of Daniel:

> We also have the prophetic message as something completely reliable, and you will do well to pay attention to it, as to a light shining in a dark place, until the day dawns and the morning star rises in your hearts. Above all, you must understand that no prophecy of Scripture came about by the prophet's own interpretation of things. For prophecy never had its origin in the human will, but prophets, though human, spoke from God as they were carried along by the Holy Spirit. (2 Peter 1:19–21)

Clearly, God gave Bible prophecy to us so that we might use it as a spotlight, shining the light of God's truth into the dark corners of this fallen world. We should not keep the truth of Bible prophecy to ourselves. We need to lift up our voices on prophetic matters as a means of shining God's light into the darkness of our sin-ridden culture and into the darkened lives of our friends, neighbors, and coworkers.

Paul, in his letter to the Ephesians, sets forth God's antidote to fear and despair. He calls it "the helmet of salvation" (Ephesians 6:17). His use of the word *salvation* doesn't refer merely to the regeneration we experience through faith in Jesus Christ. Paul also refers to salvation as "deliverance from the coming catastrophe"—a way of escape from the doom that is to come.

A helmet protects the head, the brain, the mind. One reason our culture is riddled with mindless despair is that the human mind is exposed and vulnerable to the anxieties of these dark times. No wonder mental illness is rampant in our day. We desperately need the helmet of salvation to guard our minds from the corrosive forces of this fallen world. And that is what God's prophetic Word is—a helmet of protection, God's reassurance that He is in sovereign control of human affairs.

A DREAM THAT ENDURES

The book of Daniel opens with Daniel as a young captive in Babylon. The time of the book follows the captivity of Israel when Nebuchadnezzar, the king of Babylon, took many Israelites captive to live and work in the Babylonian empire. Daniel was one of these captives, a young man of royal blood who, as a teenager, was taken away from Jerusalem.

At the conclusion of the book, we see Daniel as an old man, an honored and respected leader who has faithfully served a succession of kings of both the Babylonian and Medo-Persian Empires. Most important of all, he has faithfully served God, his one true King, throughout his life. Whenever faced with a choice of whether to obey a human king or the King of the universe, he always chose God.

In the remainder of this book, we will focus on the prophetic sections of the book of Daniel, beginning with the remarkable dream of Nebuchadnezzar, the king of Babylon, in Daniel 2. Nebuchadnezzar's dream has a nightmare quality to it. In the dream, the king sees a great image, a colossus, a statue of a man divided into five distinct sections. The head of the statue is made of gold, the chest and arms of silver, the belly and thighs of brass, the legs of iron, and the feet of a mixture of iron and clay. Nebuchadnezzar was understandably puzzled by this strange apparition. He sensed that the five sections of the statue held a deep symbolic significance—but what did they mean?

So King Nebuchadnezzar called in his wise men, enchanters, magicians, and astrologers. He demanded that they interpret the dream. As we will see, portions of that dream have already been fulfilled, but other parts of the dream are still being fulfilled in our day.

There is something ironic about the fact that we still study the dream of Nebuchadnezzar. If you were to go to modern-day Iraq, you would find the uninhabited ruins of Babylon that have been excavated on the eastern bank of the Euphrates River, about four miles north of the town of Hillah. The once-great capital of the Babylonian empire is now a field of rubble buried under desert sand. Yet the dream of Nebuchadnezzar is still preserved to be read and studied today.

Much of that dream remains to be fulfilled, so it continues to be significant to us today. We have not yet reached the end of Nebuchadnezzar's dream and its meaning. Turning to Daniel 2, we read:

> In the second year of his reign, Nebuchadnezzar had dreams; his mind was troubled and he could not sleep. So the king summoned the magicians, enchanters, sorcerers and astrologers to tell him what he had dreamed. When they came in and stood before the king, he said to them, "I have had a dream that troubles me and I want to know what it means."
>
> Then the astrologers answered the king, "May the king live forever! Tell your servants the dream, and we will interpret it."

The king replied to the astrologers, "This is what I have firmly decided: If you do not tell me what my dream was and interpret it, I will have you cut into pieces and your houses turned into piles of rubble. But if you tell me the dream and explain it, you will receive from me gifts and rewards and great honor. So tell me the dream and interpret it for me."

Once more they replied, "Let the king tell his servants the dream, and we will interpret it."

Then the king answered, "I am certain that you are trying to gain time, because you realize that this is what I have firmly decided: If you do not tell me the dream, there is only one penalty for you. You have conspired to tell me misleading and wicked things, hoping the situation will change. So then, tell me the dream, and I will know that you can interpret it for me."

The astrologers answered the king, "There is no one on earth who can do what the king asks! No king, however great and mighty, has ever asked such a thing of any magician or enchanter or astrologer. What the king asks is too difficult. No one can reveal it to the king except the gods, and they do not live among humans."

This made the king so angry and furious that he ordered the execution of all the wise men of Babylon. So the decree was issued to put the wise men to death, and men were sent to look for Daniel and his friends to put them to death. (Daniel 2:1–13)

I need to make an observation about the translation of this passage. The New International Version correctly interprets the statement by King Nebuchadnezzar to his astrologers: "This is what I have firmly decided" (v. 5). The King James Version interprets that sentence quite differently: "The thing is gone from me." In other words, the KJV suggests that the king forgot his dream when he awoke in the morning. But King Nebuchadnezzar is literally saying, "The word from me is firmly decided," meaning that King Nebuchadnezzar has firmly made up his mind how he is going to deal with his astrologers and wise men. He clearly remembers the dream and did not forget any detail of it—but to test the reliability of his mystical advisors, he is demanding that they describe the dream to him in addition to interpreting it. His astrologers claim to have supernatural insight—so let them prove it.

RIGHTEOUS SKEPTICISM

The king was wise to test his counselors in this way. He knew how easy it would be, if he spelled out the details of his dream, for the "wise men" to simply concoct a plausible sounding interpretation and claim that interpretation came from a supernatural source. Clearly, the king suspected his astrologers of being con men and frauds, perhaps because he had been fooled by them in the past.

In addition to testing his wise men, the king also motivated them, using the classic carrot-and-stick approach: "If you do not tell me what my dream was and interpret it, I will have you cut into pieces and your houses turned into piles of rubble." That was the stick. He added, "But if you tell me the dream and explain it, you will receive from me gifts and rewards and great honor." That was the carrot. If Nebuchadnezzar's advisors possessed supernatural powers, they would collect a great reward. If not, it would end badly for them.

Some people would say this is just a story about primitive people with primitive beliefs in astrology and enchantment. But look at the culture around you. Every newspaper prints a horoscope. When people meet in our society today, the first question they often ask is, "What's your sign?"—meaning, "What sign of the astrological zodiac were you born under?" Even while space observatories such as the Hubble Space Telescope are increasing our knowledge of the universe, millions still embrace the superstitious notion that the stars and planets guide their individual destinies.

A number of years ago, I was interviewed on a radio talk show. In the course of the interview, the host asked my opinion of a certain well-known woman who wrote books and made media appearances, foretelling future events by means of astrology. It was clear that this radio host had a high regard for this fortune-teller. "We recently had her as our guest," he told me on the air, "and she said some amazing things about the future."

Because of his earnest praise for the woman, I realized I had to tread carefully. So I said, "I'm not in a position to judge this woman and her motives. But I do know this: She has openly admitted she is often wrong in her prognostications. I know many people are impressed when she bats five hundred. Personally, I don't consider that an impressive batting average. What impresses me is that the Word of God is always 100 percent right. The Bible has made many predictions, and it has always batted a thousand. When the Bible makes a prediction, it hits it on the nose every time."

Again and again, the Scriptures tell us we should be righteous skeptics. We should never take any so-called "prophet" at face value, but we should test that "prophet" to make sure he or she speaks for God, as prompted by God's Spirit. One of the tests of a true prophet is that he always bats a thousand. A true prophet is never wrong. That principle was announced by the prophet Jeremiah when he opposed the false prophet Hananiah in Jeremiah 28:1–13. A prophet, he said, "will be recognized as one truly sent by the LORD only if his prediction comes true" (v. 9). Other tests of true and false prophets are listed in Deuteronomy 13:1–5; 18:20; Matthew 7:15–20; and 1 John 4:1–3.

A VISION OF FUTURE EVENTS

King Nebuchadnezzar's skepticism toward his astrologers and enchanters is well founded. He challenges them to tell him his dream and interpret it, but they are unable to do so. So he proceeds to carry out his threat and orders the execution of the so-called "wise men" of Babylon. He issues a decree to execute them all, including Daniel and his friends. Here we rejoin Daniel's narrative:

> When Arioch, the commander of the king's guard, had gone out to put to death the wise men of Babylon, Daniel spoke to him with wisdom and tact. He asked the king's officer, "Why did the king issue such a harsh decree?" Arioch then explained the matter to Daniel. At this, Daniel went in to the king and asked for time, so that he might interpret the dream for him.
>
> Then Daniel returned to his house and explained the matter to his friends Hananiah, Mishael and Azariah. He urged them to plead for mercy from the God of heaven concerning this mystery, so that he and his friends might not be executed with the rest of the wise men of Babylon. During the night the mystery was revealed to Daniel in a vision. Then Daniel praised the God of heaven and said:
>
>> "Praise be to the name of God for ever and ever;
>>> wisdom and power are his.
>> He changes times and seasons;
>>> he deposes kings and raises up others.
>> He gives wisdom to the wise
>>> and knowledge to the discerning.
>> He reveals deep and hidden things;
>>> he knows what lies in darkness,
>>> and light dwells with him.
>> I thank and praise you, God of my ancestors:
>>> You have given me wisdom and power,
>> you have made known to me what we asked of you,
>>> you have made known to us the dream of the king."
>
> Then Daniel went to Arioch, whom the king had appointed to execute the wise men of Babylon, and said

to him, "Do not execute the wise men of Babylon. Take me to the king, and I will interpret his dream for him."

Arioch took Daniel to the king at once and said, "I have found a man among the exiles from Judah who can tell the king what his dream means." (Daniel 2:14–25)

We can clearly see, between the lines, that the hand of God is moving in these events, orchestrating everything—the king's dream, the skepticism of the king toward his astrologers, and even the threat to the lives of Daniel and his friends. It is all part of a master plan to elevate Daniel and place him in a position of responsibility in service to the Babylonian king. When King Nebuchadnezzar sends his executioner to take Daniel into custody, Daniel makes his appeal: "Take me to the king, and I will interpret his dream for him." So Arioch, the executioner, takes Daniel into the presence of the king:

The king asked Daniel (also called Belteshazzar), "Are you able to tell me what I saw in my dream and interpret it?"

Daniel replied, "No wise man, enchanter, magician or diviner can explain to the king the mystery he has asked about, but there is a God in heaven who reveals mysteries. He has shown King Nebuchadnezzar what will happen in days to come." (Daniel 2:26–28)

Here Daniel uses a phrase that is truly the key to this dream and to the entire book of Daniel. It is the phrase "in days to come," or as some translations put it, "in the latter days." The prophet Daniel tells King Nebuchadnezzar that God has revealed to him a vision of future events. Daniel goes on to say:

"Your dream and the visions that passed through your mind as you were lying in bed are these:

"As Your Majesty was lying there, your mind turned to things to come, and the revealer of mysteries showed you what is going to happen. As for me, this mystery has been revealed to me, not because I have greater wisdom than anyone else alive, but so that Your Majesty may know the interpretation and that you may understand what went through your mind." (Daniel 2:28–30)

So Daniel makes it plain to the king that he has experienced a vision of future events—both the near future and the far distant future.

DOES THE BOOK OF DANIEL
LOOK FORWARD—OR BACKWARD?

Do the prophecies of Daniel truly predict events that were in Daniel's future? Critics of the Bible have attacked the book of Daniel on this very question.

Because critics of the Bible do not accept the possibility of the miraculous or the validity of prophecy, they make an *a priori* assumption that the predictive element in the book of Daniel is a lie. These same critics also attack the virgin birth and the resurrection of Jesus. Assuming that such events *cannot* occur, they deny that such events have *ever* occurred, and they conclude that the biblical account is a fabrication and a fable. To base a conclusion on a preconceived bias is not rational, and these critics often find themselves in the position of simply denying solid historical evidence because the evidence doesn't fit their prejudice.

How do the critics explain the fact that Nebuchadnezzar's dream, as interpreted by the prophet Daniel, predicts with uncanny accuracy events that occurred centuries later? They simply ascribe a later date to the book of Daniel! Instead of dating the writing of the book at about 600 BC, as the internal evidence suggests, the critics insist that the book was composed much later, around 165 BC, or about two centuries after the events prophetically described in the dream. In other words, the critics claim the dream is not a prediction but a fabrication composed *after* the historical events took place.

But there's a major problem with the late-date view of the book of Daniel. In the late 1940s and early 1950s, the Dead Sea Scrolls were discovered in a dozen caves at Wadi Qumran near the Dead Sea, in what is now the West Bank. Archaeologists date the scrolls as having been inscribed around 125 BC. Among the scrolls were portions of two copies of the book of Daniel. Bible scholars consider it next to impossible that the book of Daniel could have been composed as late as 165 BC, then be revered as Scripture a mere forty years later.

One Bible scholar, Dr. Edward J. Young, observed that the discovery of the Daniel scrolls "is most striking, for it apparently shows that two copies of the book were in circulation very shortly after the alleged time of its composition. It begins to look as though this consideration will make more difficult the maintaining of a late date for the authorship of the prophecy of Daniel." And Dead Sea Scrolls scholar Walter E. Wegner noted that even Oxford philologist G. R. Driver—a longtime advocate of the late-date theory—was forced by the evidence to admit that "the presence and popularity of the Daniel manuscripts at Qumran conflicts with the modern view" of a late composition date for Daniel.[1]

It is practically inconceivable that the book of Daniel could have been regarded as sacred Scripture by the Essenes (the ancient Jewish sect that hid the scrolls in the caves) if the book of Daniel had been composed that recently. In order to be so widely accepted and distributed as part of the sacred canon of Scripture, the book of Daniel had to have been composed centuries earlier than the critics claim. So the most likely explanation is that the book of Daniel truly was written around 600 BC, and it prophetically describes events that would not take place until centuries later.

THE LATTER DAYS

The phrase "in days to come" (or "in the latter days") concerns itself with a particular aspect of the future known as "the end times," or "the last days." In various forms, this phrase appears in a number of places in the Old Testament. One instance is found in the prophecy of Hosea. In Hosea 3, the prophet gathers up the entire history of Israel following the nation's captivity in Babylon and says:

> For the Israelites will live many days without king or prince, without sacrifice or sacred stones, without ephod or household gods. Afterward the Israelites will return and seek the LORD their God and David their king. They will come trembling to the LORD and to his blessings in the last days. (Hosea 3:4–5)

It's clear that when Hosea says the Israelites will live for many days without sacrifice, he is prophesying about a time *after* the earthly ministry of our Lord. We know this because in the New Testament we see that the Jewish people were still sacrificing in the temple in Jerusalem. Hosea predicts that the time will come when Israel will no longer be able to make sacrifices in the temple. When was Hosea's prophecy fulfilled? Its fulfillment began in AD 70, when the Roman general Titus Flavius besieged and conquered Jerusalem. The Roman army utterly demolished the temple, which was being used by Jewish rebels to make their last stand.

Almost two thousand years after that event, the conditions Hosea described are still in force. The Jewish people are still without a temple and still without a blood sacrifice. Hosea's prophecy goes on to tell us that the people of Israel shall turn to God and to "David their king" (an apparent reference to Jesus, the King of the Jews, the Son of David), and they will return "trembling to the LORD and to his blessings in the last days" (v. 5).

In the original Hebrew language, both of these verses—Daniel 2:28 and Hosea 3:5—use the same identical phrase for "in days to come," or "in the last days." That Hebrew phrase is *'achariyth yowm*. This is a phrase that, throughout the Old Testament, is used to refer to the end times—and specifically the end of the times of the

Gentiles. This confirms that the dream of King Nebuchadnezzar is a prophecy that concerns itself with the end times that still lie ahead of us in the future.

This prediction in Daniel 2 takes on increased significance for us in view of our Lord's words about Jerusalem. Forty years before Jerusalem was destroyed by the Romans, Jesus spoke these remarkable words: "Jerusalem will be trampled on by the Gentiles until the times of the Gentiles are fulfilled" (Luke 21:24).

Jesus was saying that Jerusalem would be under the control and occupation of Gentile overlords, and the Jews would never again possess the city until the times of the Gentiles should be fulfilled. It is remarkable to me that this prophecy of our Lord began to be fulfilled in my own times, on June 6, 1967, when the Israelis recaptured Jerusalem in the course of the Six-Day War.

It's a moving experience to visit Jerusalem and see Jews thronging the streets of the Old City once again. Orthodox Jews with their long curly sideburns and their unusual hats and garments stand and gaze longingly into the temple courts. Few Jews are allowed access, and they are not allowed to pray there. Each Sabbath, they gather at the Western Wall in great numbers. They run through the streets of the city in order to be present at the beginning of the service to remember Jerusalem's glory, and they wail over her present desolation. In light of the Lord's words, the Jewish recapture of Jerusalem indicates that we have reached the last of the times of the Gentiles.

We should note that, in the Lord's phrase "until the times of the Gentiles are fulfilled," the word *times* (*kairoi* in the original Greek) is an inaccurate translation. A better translation would be *season*. We see this distinction in Acts 1:7 (KJV), where Jesus tells His followers, "It is not for you to know the times [Greek *chronous*] or the seasons [*kairous*], which the Father hath put in his own power."

When the Bible speaks of "times," it refers to great overall divisions of time in which God is working out His major purposes in human history. For example, the apostle Paul spoke of "the times of this ignorance" (see Acts 17:30 KJV), which refers to the entire

Old Testament period, before the arrival of Jesus the Messiah. These broad expanses of time are, in turn, divided into "seasons," shorter divisions characterized by specific events or developments within the broader time periods, much as we refer to the seasons of the year.

In his book *Synonyms of the New Testament*, Archbishop Richard Trench explains how God's seasons function within the broader scope of God's times: "The seasons (*kairoi*) are the joints or articulations in these times, the critical epoch-making periods foreordained of God . . . when all that has been slowly, and often without observation, ripening through long ages is mature and comes to the birth in grand decisive events, which constitute at once the close of one period and the commencement of another."[2]

If we place June 6, 1967, when the Israelis recaptured Jerusalem, into the context Archbishop Trench describes, we see that it is a "grand decisive event" that marks the close of one period (season) and the commencement of another. If we are correct in this view, then the last "season" in which Gentile authority will reign unchallenged in the world has already begun.

Who knows how long this season will last? We cannot set dates. There are no limitations on how long these seasons take to run their course. But according to our Lord's own prediction, the last of the seasons of the Gentiles has already begun.

THE DREAM REVEALED AND INTERPRETED

Within this lengthy period called "the times of the Gentiles," which began with Nebuchadnezzar, this dream of the king (as interpreted by Daniel) indicates that there would be four world powers, and only four. Let's listen in as Daniel speaks to Nebuchadnezzar and reveals and interprets the king's dream:

> "Your Majesty looked, and there before you stood a large statue—an enormous, dazzling statue, awesome in appearance. The head of the statue was made of pure

gold, its chest and arms of silver, its belly and thighs of bronze, its legs of iron, and its feet partly of iron and partly of baked clay. While you were watching, a rock was cut out, but not by human hands. It struck the statue on its feet of iron and clay and smashed them. Then the iron, the clay, the bronze, the silver and the gold were all broken to pieces and became like chaff on a threshing floor in the summer. The wind swept them away without leaving a trace. But the rock that struck the statue became a huge mountain and filled the whole earth.

"This was the dream, and now we will interpret it to the king. Your Majesty, you are the king of kings. The God of heaven has given you dominion and power and might and glory; in your hands he has placed all mankind and the beasts of the field and the birds in the sky. Wherever they live, he has made you ruler over them all. You are that head of gold.

"After you, another kingdom will arise, inferior to yours. Next, a third kingdom, one of bronze, will rule over the whole earth. Finally, there will be a fourth kingdom, strong as iron—for iron breaks and smashes everything—and as iron breaks things to pieces, so it will crush and break all the others. Just as you saw that the feet and toes were partly of baked clay and partly of iron, so this will be a divided kingdom; yet it will have some of the strength of iron in it, even as you saw iron mixed with clay. As the toes were partly iron and partly clay, so this kingdom will be partly strong and partly brittle. And just as you saw the iron mixed with baked clay, so the people will be a mixture and will not remain united, any more than iron mixes with clay.

"In the time of those kings, the God of heaven will set up a kingdom that will never be destroyed, nor will it be left to another people. It will crush all those kingdoms and bring them to an end, but it will itself endure forever. This is the meaning of the vision of the rock cut out of a mountain, but not by human hands—a rock that broke the iron, the bronze, the clay, the silver and the gold to pieces.

"The great God has shown the king what will take place in the future. The dream is true and its interpretation is trustworthy." (Daniel 2:31–45)

Four world powers are indicated by a head of gold, the chest and arms of silver, the midsection of brass, and the legs of iron. The fifth division, the feet composed of mingled iron and clay, is a picture of mingled strength and weakness, because iron and clay do not mix. Daniel tells us that the golden head represents Babylon, the empire ruled by King Nebuchadnezzar.

The Babylonian kingdom would be followed, Daniel says, by a second kingdom that would be inferior to the first, represented in the dream by the chest and arms of silver. History identifies this second kingdom for us. In fact, the second kingdom appears on the scene even before the book of Daniel closes. At the end of the book, Daniel is no longer under the Babylonian Empire but is now serving under the Medo-Persian Empire (also known as the Achaemenid Empire), a powerful but divided kingdom composed of the older Median confederation and the newer Persian Empire ruled by Cyrus the Great. The Medo-Persian Empire conquered the Babylonian Empire and succeeded it as the dominant kingdom of the world.

The Medo-Persian Empire would be followed by a third empire, represented by the midsection of brass. This third kingdom appears on the scene very quickly and expands rapidly. Later, in Daniel 8, the prophet Daniel experiences a vision, and Daniel mentions this third kingdom by name: Greece (see Daniel 8:21). History confirms that the Greek Empire came to dominate the world under the leadership of Alexander the Great, who ruled from 336 to 323 BC. Alexander conquered Asia Minor, the Middle East, Egypt, Persia, and part of the Indian subcontinent by the time of his mysterious and agonizing death (possibly due to poisoning) at the early age of thirty-two.

Next, we come to the fourth empire, represented by the legs of iron. This fourth empire is of central importance to our study. In Daniel's account, it is a strange and mysterious kingdom that arises to succeed the kingdom of Greece. Most Bible scholars identify this fourth empire as the Roman Empire, which was certainly an empire of iron rule.

This fourth kingdom *includes* the Roman Empire at the very least—of that there is no doubt. Certain predictive passages in the New Testament make it very clear that this fourth kingdom had its beginnings in Rome. In Revelation 17, the apostle John describes his vision of a great power he identifies as "BABYLON THE GREAT, THE MOTHER OF PROSTITUTES AND OF THE ABOMINATIONS OF THE EARTH," and he identifies "Babylon" as being founded on seven hills (see Revelation 17:9). For centuries, the city of Rome has been known as "The City of Seven Hills." There can be little doubt that this fourth kingdom, the iron kingdom that is centrally important in both the book of Daniel and the book of Revelation, had its beginnings in the city of Rome.

It's important to remember that the period represented by the image in the dream covers all of history from the age of Nebuchadnezzar to the second coming of Jesus Christ. Therefore, the legs of iron that represent the fourth kingdom must include far more than the Roman Empire. That's why the Roman Empire is never so named in the Bible. We would be much closer to an accurate identification of this fourth kingdom if we referred to it as "Western civilization" or "the Western nations." All of Western civilization—the artistic, philosophical, and cultural heritage of Europe, the traditions of the Middle Ages, Renaissance, and Enlightenment, the scientific revolution—all of these cultural trends can be traced back to Rome. Moreover, these traditions were exported to America by European colonialism.

This is the time of the Gentiles that Jesus spoke of, a time that began drawing to a close on June 6, 1967, when the Israelis recaptured and began to reoccupy the city of Jerusalem. Since then, the culture of the Gentiles, the culture of Western civilization, has been in decline, even though the people in the Western nations have been largely unaware of it. This prophecy focuses on what will happen to these nations, especially as they near the end.

In the next chapter, we will explore in greater detail what Daniel reveals about Western civilization and its remarkable place in the processes of history. But before we move on to that study, I want to point out one notable fact about the image in King Nebuchadnezzar's dream. As you look at the sections of the image, you see a decreasing value of the metals from the head to the feet. It begins with gold, then silver, then bronze and, finally, common iron. As these metals decrease in value, their strength increases. Gold is soft and malleable, but iron, though cheap and common, is hard and strong. But when the final stage is reached, there is a mingling of iron and clay—and in that mingling of materials, there is no strength at all.

It's important to understand that Nebuchadnezzar was the most autocratic king ever to rule in all the world. Daniel says that God gave Nebuchadnezzar authority over all the earth, and he had the right to rule over all the world. No one ever withstood him. Nebuchadnezzar's successors were finally overthrown by the Medo-Persian Empire, as Daniel had predicted, but Nebuchadnezzar himself was never defeated or overthrown.

As citizens of the Western world, you and I are accustomed to thinking of a democratic republic as the most perfect form of government. But the dream of King Nebuchadnezzar indicates that, in God's sight, the most perfect form of government is not a democracy but a monarchy. A monarchy is headed by a single individual whose will is the law throughout the length and breadth of his kingdom. As monarch, Nebuchadnezzar symbolized God's ideal of the best kind of government, even though Nebuchadnezzar the man was far from God's ideal monarch (as other events in the book of Daniel clearly show).

The virtue and justice of a monarchy is directly related to the character of the individual who occupies the throne. Flawed human kings result in flawed human governments. But a day is coming when God's kingdom will prevail over all the earth with the right monarch on the throne—the Lord Jesus Christ. That's why Paul refers to God as "the blessed and only Ruler, the King of kings and Lord of lords" (1 Timothy 6:15) who will one day reign over the earth.

A FIRM FOUNDATION

The most remarkable feature of Nebuchadnezzar's dream is not these four human kingdoms but the strange and final kingdom that arises in the end. This kingdom begins when a rock, not cut by human hands, strikes the iron-and-clay feet of the statue, smashing them. The statue collapses into pieces, and the rubble is swept away on the wind, leaving no trace. But the rock itself becomes a vast mountain that fills the whole earth. This mountain that grows from the rock symbolizes what the Bible declares: All the kingdoms of men will end at the appearing of God's kingdom. Then the prayer that Jesus taught us to pray will be fulfilled: ". . . your kingdom come, your will be done, on earth as it is in heaven" (Matthew 6:10).

This is our great hope: Our King and His kingdom are coming! This great truth should focus our minds and alter the way we look at life. It should impact the way we invest our time and our talent. Are we pouring our lives into earthly kingdoms that are doomed to fail—or are we investing in the kingdom that will stand forever? Are we spending our lives on that which perishes or that which lasts?

The Bible does not prohibit us from making investments in earthly affairs, but it does urge that we organize our lives according to spiritual reality. Do not become too deeply mired in the things of this world. Don't waste your life on material things that will ultimately pass away. Hold the things of this world loosely, and invest in what will last.

This is what Jesus meant when He said, "Do not store up for yourselves treasures on earth, where moths and vermin destroy, and where thieves break in and steal. But store up for yourselves treasures in heaven, where moths and vermin do not destroy, and where thieves do not break in and steal. For where your treasure is, there your heart will be also" (Matthew 6:19–21).

God has set these prophetic passages of Scripture before us so that we can see what matters—and what doesn't. The fatal flaw in all human kingdoms is that they are built upon a false foundation. In Matthew 7, Jesus gave the example of two houses, one built on a foundation of rock and the other on a foundation of sand. The house built on sand collapsed when the rains came and the winds beat against it, but the house built on rock could not be moved.

The kingdoms of the earth, the kingdoms of Western civilization, are doomed to decline and fall. They are all built on sand. But the coming kingdom of God on earth will be built on the unshakable foundation of Jesus, the Rock of our faith.

The greatest tragedy I can imagine would be to arrive at the end of life and discover that, in the judgment of our sovereign God, we have wasted the life He gave us. This prophecy was given to us so that we could measure our lives and learn to distinguish between the temporary and the eternal, between the passing and the permanent. May God grant wisdom and understanding as we continue to study this book and discover His plan for the days ahead.

3

THE LAST ACT

Daniel 2:40–49

The book of Daniel comes with the highest recommendation imaginable—the recommendation of the Lord Jesus himself. As He sat with His disciples on the Mount of Olives, overlooking Jerusalem, He told them:

> "So when you see standing in the holy place 'the abomination that causes desolation,' spoken of through the prophet Daniel—let the reader understand—then let those who are in Judea flee to the mountains. . . . For then there will be great distress, unequaled from the beginning of the world until now—and never to be equaled again." (Matthew 24:15–16, 21)

By these words, Jesus indicated that there is considerable profit to be gained by studying the book of Daniel. We are still examining Daniel 2 and the amazing dream image that was first beheld by King Nebuchadnezzar of Babylon and interpreted for him by Daniel the prophet. In this dream, Nebuchadnezzar saw a towering image, a statue with the head of gold, chest and arms of silver, midsection of bronze, legs of iron, and feet of mingled iron and clay. This image presented in symbolic form a grand outline of history into which all other prophetic passages of the Old and New Testaments can be placed.

Our task is to investigate Daniel's interpretation of this dream, with a special focus on the fourth division, the kingdom of iron. As we previously saw, the first three divisions of the image have already been fulfilled in history, and they were fulfilled exactly according to the pattern predicted by Daniel. The head of gold was the empire of Babylon; the chest and arms of silver represented the divided kingdom of Medo-Persia; the belly and thighs of bronze represented the conquering kingdom of Alexander the Great, the youthful conqueror who (it is said) wept when he realized there were no other worlds to conquer.

Finally, there was the fourth kingdom, the empire of iron that had its origins in the city of Rome. It is this fourth kingdom that is vitally important to you and me, because we still live in the fourth kingdom to this day. As Daniel tells us in his interpretation of Nebuchadnezzar's dream, the fourth kingdom appeared on the scene as the empire of Greece was in decline. This fourth kingdom—which represents all of Western civilization—will last until God sets up His own kingdom on earth.

CHARACTERISTICS OF THE "IRON KINGDOM"

As we focus on this fourth kingdom, several matters of intense interest arrest our attention. Let's listen as Daniel speaks to King Nebuchadnezzar about this fourth kingdom:

> "Finally, there will be a fourth kingdom, strong as iron—
> for iron breaks and smashes everything—and as iron
> breaks things to pieces, so it will crush and break all the
> others." (Daniel 2:40)

This prophecy must have seemed darkly mysterious to Nebuchadnezzar. He could not imagine what this fourth kingdom would look like or where it would arise. But history has a way of clarifying and interpreting prophetic mysteries. These words of Daniel are much more meaningful to us today, in the twenty-first century, than they were to King Nebuchadnezzar. In fact, even those who read the prophecy of Daniel in the first century, during the time of the Lord's earthly ministry, would have realized that the fourth kingdom, the kingdom of iron, began with the Roman Empire.

Three hundred years before Christ, the city-state of Rome, situated on the banks of the Tiber River in Italy, had already come to dominate the city-states and tribes of Italy. The nascent Roman nation had begun to assert its power, spreading its influence into the Mediterranean world. Roman legions conquered territory throughout Italy and across southern France and down into Spain. Roman ships crossed the Mediterranean and landed forces in North Africa. Roman armies clashed with the forces of Carthage and fought their way across Egypt, across Greece, and across the Middle East.

By the time Jesus was born, the Roman Empire had become the dominant political and military power of earth. From our historical vantage point, we can clearly see why the Roman Empire was symbolized as a kingdom of iron in Nebuchadnezzar's dream. As the prophet Daniel said, "Iron breaks things to pieces, so it will crush and break all the others." Anyone who has read the story of the Roman Empire knows that it was the nature of the Roman military to break and crush and shatter its opponents into submission. The Romans were seized by an overriding passion to rule the world, and they overwhelmed all opposition by utilizing the short sword, which became the trademark of the Roman soldier.

In *The Story of Civilization*, Will and Ariel Durant tell us that the Roman Senate sometimes deliberately began wars in order to acquire wealth for Rome or to quiet unrest among the plebeians and slaves at home. The Roman legions brutally imposed what came to be called "the Pax Romana," the peace of Rome, a peace imposed by military might, political oppression, and outright terror. The lands that came under Roman rule were stable and orderly because any unrest or rebellion was quickly and brutally put down.

Another characteristic of the "iron kingdom" of Rome is that it has stamped its image upon the entire Western world. The Roman culture was marked by a passion for establishing far-flung colonies, then defending those colonies by military might. That peculiar characteristic of the Roman Empire has characterized the entire history of Western civilization. Western nations have established colonies all around the world—and the establishment of colonies created the necessity for great navies and armies to protect the trade routes and colonies against attack. As a result, the Western nations became powerful and highly militarized in order to protect the colonies they established.

Over time, the Roman Empire became divided between East and West. These divisions corresponded to the two legs of iron in the image of Nebuchadnezzar's dream. The western half of the empire was centered in Rome. The eastern half of the empire, with Constantinople as its capital, became the Byzantine Empire. The Byzantine Empire planted colonies northward into Russia and eastward into Persia (Iran) and Mesopotamia (Iraq). Thus it spread the Byzantine culture across the eastern world.

The Western Roman Empire, centered in Rome, spread its colonies around the Mediterranean, across western Europe, and up into Britain. Even after the fall of Rome itself, the Roman culture continued to dominate as the kingdoms of Europe arose—the monarchies of Portugal, Spain, France, Italy, Germany, Belgium, and Britain. These monarchies built fleets and sent their ships out into the world to bring back treasures and slaves.

Spain and Portugal were the two great colonial powers of the fifteenth and sixteenth centuries, sending forth explorers and conquerors throughout the world. Portugal sent Bartolomeu Dias to the southern tip of Africa, Vasco da Gama to India, and Pedro Álvares Cabral to Brazil. Spain sent Christopher Columbus out to discover and colonize a new world, which became known as America.

In the seventeenth century, England arose as the chief rival to Spain and Portugal in the New World. France and the Netherlands also established colonial empires during this era—and many of those colonies were in the Western Hemisphere.

With a look back through history, we can see that every nation that established a colony in the Western Hemisphere was once itself a colony of the Roman Empire. Our entire Western world is Roman to the core.

We see evidence of Roman influence in our own history, in the structure of our own government. Our United States Senate, a fundamental institution of our government, is copied directly from the Roman Senate. Our republican form of government is based on the Republic of Rome. Our courts, our laws, and our military structure are all heavily influenced by those same features of the Roman Empire. Our national symbol, the American bald eagle, was suggested to the founding fathers by the Roman *aquila,* a golden standard in the shape of an eagle that was carried into battle by Roman legions. Our government buildings in Washington D.C. are based on Roman architecture.

So when we envision the "iron kingdom" of the Roman Empire, we have to acknowledge that we in America are part of that "iron kingdom" as well.

THE DECLINE OF GENTILE CIVILIZATION

If you are a student of history, you'll recall that the Vandals, Visigoths, and other pagan Germanic tribes from the north swept down over the Alps and overran Italy. This invasion culminated in the Sack of Rome in August 410. The pillaging of the "Eternal City" prompted St. Jerome, who then lived in Bethlehem, to write that Rome was besieged and her citizens were forced to buy their lives with gold. "My voice sticks in my throat," he wrote, "and, as I dictate, sobs choke my utterance. The City which had taken the whole world was itself taken."[1]

The old Roman Empire of the Caesars crumbled and collapsed. Out of this chaos emerged a religious and political institution known as the Holy Roman Empire—the empire of the institutional Church. The Roman Catholic Church became a stabilizing influence throughout the region that had once been conquered and controlled by the iron-fisted Roman Empire. The pope ultimately emerged as a Roman ruler. The empire was still Roman in its character, but it was now a religious empire. The seat of imperial government was transferred to France, then into Spain, and finally to Germany.

The Germans called their ruler the "Kaiser," which is the German transliteration of Caesar. In this way, the heritage of the Roman Caesars was perpetuated into the twentieth century, when the imperialistic ambition of Kaiser Wilhelm of Germany was a key factor in igniting World War I.

A strikingly similar chain of events took place in the remnant of the Eastern Roman Empire under the Byzantines. In 1453, the Byzantine capital city, Constantinople, was sacked by the northern tribes. The seat of government was moved from Constantinople to Russia. The Russian ruler was called the "Czar," which is the Russian spelling of Caesar. Thus the heritage of the Roman Caesars was perpetuated into the twentieth century through imperial Russia as well as through imperial Germany.

And here is a fascinating historical footnote: Both divisions of the Roman Empire, the Western division (centered in Germany, embodied in the Kaiser) and the Eastern division (centered in Russia, embodied in the Czar) ended in the same year, 1918. In July 1918, the Russian Czar—bloody Nicholas II of the Romanov dynasty, who abdicated the previous March in the wake of the Russian Revolution—was executed by the Bolsheviks. And in November 1918, Kaiser Wilhelm, the last German Emperor and King of Prussia, abdicated and fled into exile in the Netherlands.

So we see that remnants of the old Roman Empire were still shaping events into the twentieth century. And through the United States and other Western nations, the influence of the old Roman Empire continues to be felt around the world, on into the twenty-first century. Western civilization is stamped with the Roman image. It has only recently ceased to colonize and dominate major parts of the earth. The mighty fourth kingdom, the iron kingdom that Daniel said would dominate the earth, still lives today—though its power is waning.

The great Western military power that defeated imperialism and totalitarianism in World War I and World War II has appeared vulnerable in Vietnam and Afghanistan—wars that have been fought since Jerusalem was retaken by the Israelis in June 1967. Could it be that the defeat of Western military might in recent years might be additional signs that the times of the Gentiles are being fulfilled, as the Lord predicted in Luke 21:24? Could it be that other signs of the approaching collapse of Western civilization—economic decline, the global debt crisis, the loss of technological and commercial dominance in the world, the moral and spiritual decay of Western culture, the expanding entitlement mentality and the growth of the welfare state—also point to the end of the times of the Gentiles and the fulfillment of the Lord's prophecy?

Are we approaching the end of the reign of the kingdom of iron?

IRON MINGLED WITH CLAY

In verse 41, a strange and remarkable new element enters the picture. Daniel says to King Nebuchadnezzar:

> "Just as you saw that the feet and toes were partly of baked clay and partly of iron, so this will be a divided kingdom; yet it will have some of the strength of iron in it, even as you saw iron mixed with clay." (Daniel 2:41)

We previously saw that the fourth kingdom, represented by the legs of iron, became divided between a Western empire and an Eastern empire, the Roman Empire and the Byzantine Empire. Here in this verse, however, we see a different division—a division not by geography, but by character. This division becomes apparent at the foot stage of the image. Though the legs were made of solid iron, Daniel saw that the feet of the image were made of mingled iron and clay.

What does the mingling of iron and clay symbolize? Clay is the opposite of iron. Iron speaks of an imperialistic attitude, characterized by power and might, conquering and ruling by brute force. By contrast, clay is soft, pliable, and easily molded. Many Bible scholars have identified the clay in this image as the principle of democracy—and I agree with that view.

This statement may cause you to bristle. Most Western nations have democratic governments, and most Westerners dislike hearing democracy attacked. Though we are all aware of certain inefficiencies and problems that arise from democratic government, we generally tend to agree with Winston Churchill, who, in a speech before the House of Commons, November 11, 1947, said, "Many forms of Government have been tried, and will be tried in this world of sin and woe. No one pretends that democracy is perfect or all wise. Indeed, it has been said that democracy is the worst form of Government except all those other forms that have been tried from time to time."[2]

We like to think that the reason the United States has been economically and militarily secure is its democratic government. We want to believe that it is the voice of the people that gives a nation its strength and wisdom. But if you look at history, especially the history of the West, you discover that democracy is not really a very good form of government. This is especially true in light of the revelation of God's Word.

The voice of the people has always been a fickle voice, easily shaped and molded like the clay in Nebuchadnezzar's dream. Politicians count on being able to sway public opinion, either through appeals to emotion, appeals to selfishness and greed, or appeals to fear and irrational hatred. Politicians who exploit the prejudices and ignorance of less thoughtful, less educated voters are called *demagogues*. These people are extremely dangerous because they know how to exploit the fundamental weakness in any democracy, which is that people will eagerly give power to those who promise the most and who appeal to the lowest common denominator of human nature. Demagogues have never been more dangerous than they are today in our mass-media age.

There is a quotation that, at least as far back as the early 1950s, has been attributed to Alexander Fraser Tytler (1747–1813), a Scottish historian at the University of Edinburgh. We now know that this quotation does not appear in any of Tytler's writings, and we do not know who the actual author was. It matters little who first wrote these words; what does matter is that history has proven these words to be wise and true:

> A democracy cannot exist as a permanent form of government. It can only exist until the voters discover that they can vote themselves largesse from the public treasury. From that moment on, the majority always votes for the candidates promising the most benefits from the public treasury with the result that a democracy always collapses over loose fiscal policy, always followed by a dictatorship.[3]

We are seeing the truth of this statement borne out in our own time. As the entitlement state expands, as fewer and fewer people pay into the system, voters increasingly vote themselves more benefits from the public treasury. Demagogues empower themselves and purchase votes with money from the public treasury. As the government distributes more wealth than it takes in, the debt grows to a level that is unsustainable—and the democracy collapses of its own unsustainable weight.

RIPE FOR INVASION

It wasn't democracy that made America great. The source of America's greatness is righteousness. There is another quotation, often misattributed to Alexis de Tocqueville. Again, the actual author of the words is unknown, but the wisdom of the words is unimpeachable: "America is great because she is good, and if America ever ceases to be good, she will cease to be great." When righteousness pervades a nation, the people are strong; when righteousness departs, the people falter. That is why our American democracy has begun to stagger and crumble. Righteousness is evaporating from America, and America's greatness is evaporating with it.

Proverbs 14:34 tells us, "Righteousness exalts a nation, but sin condemns any people." A parallel statement is found in the state motto of Hawaii, which reads in the Hawaiian Polynesian language, "Ua Mau ke Ea o ka 'Āina i ka Pono," or, "The life of the land is perpetuated in righteousness," words spoken in 1843 by Hawaii's King Kamehameha III. Righteousness, not democracy, is the fundamental secret of America's strength.

In this passage, the prophet Daniel says the kingdom will be divided between the iron strength of imperial rule and the soft clay of democracy. The Western nations, in their final stages of decline, will be dominated by the Roman power principle but undermined by democratic principles. Those final stages will witness a struggle between two principles: the iron of imperialism and the clay of democracy. The outcome of that struggle will be weakness and decline, not strength.

World War I marked the beginning of the end of an era. The end of that war was marked by the fall of crowned heads across the world. Many monarchies ended abruptly or were transformed into representative monarchies in which the monarch became a mere figurehead, exercising no authority at all.

World War II completed this transition. The age of kings ended during the interim between the wars. At the same time, a new age emerged, as Daniel goes on to describe for us:

> "As the toes were partly iron and partly clay, so this king-
> dom will be partly strong and partly brittle. And just as

you saw the iron mixed with baked clay, so the people will
be a mixture and will not remain united, any more than
iron mixes with clay." (Daniel 2:42–43)

It's chilling to compare this verse with the current events we read
about and watch on our TV and computer screens. What is happening in the nations of the West in our day? They are torn by domestic
strife. Though outwardly strong, they are inwardly weakened by
social and political conflict. Our Western democracies boast of their
great military might, their bustling financial centers with towering
skyscrapers, and their global commerce. Outwardly, the Western
democracies seem as strong and unbreakable as iron.

But the souls of the people are spiritually and morally depleted.
The governments of these nations are financially depleted and stag-
gering under a load of unsustainable debt. There is continual strife
between classes, races, cultures, and political philosophies. All of
these forces, ideologies, and conflicting interests are pulling at the
fabric of Western society.

In spite of the illusion of outward strength, our Western democracies are inwardly weak and as soft as clay. The democratic voice
of the people and the iron will of governmental authority are in
conflict. This mingling of iron and clay has set the stage for the
final act of history.

The world is ripe for the invasion of God.

THE STONE THAT INVADES HUMAN HISTORY

Next, the prophet Daniel discloses to King Nebuchadnezzar the
final act in the drama of human history:

"In the time of those kings, the God of heaven will set
up a kingdom that will never be destroyed, nor will it be
left to another people. It will crush all those kingdoms
and bring them to an end, but it will itself endure forever.

This is the meaning of the vision of the rock cut out of a mountain, but not by human hands—a rock that broke the iron, the bronze, the clay, the silver and the gold to pieces.

"The great God has shown the king what will take place in the future. The dream is true and its interpretation is trustworthy." (Daniel 2:44–45)

Notice the opening phrase: "In the time of those kings . . ." Who are the kings Daniel refers to? In the interpretation of this dream, Daniel has referred to kingdoms but not kings. So this reference seems cryptic.

But if you compare this passage with a parallel passage in Daniel 7 and with the book of Revelation, Daniel's meaning becomes clear. He is referring to the final form of the Western confederacy of nations that will emerge from the iron kingdom. These ten nations are represented by the ten toes of the image. The phrase "those kings" can only refer to the leaders of the ten nations or kingdoms making up the fourth kingdom in its final form. These ten nations are essentially Roman in form and structure. When God establishes his kingdom, those ten nations will be destroyed.

In the king's dream, a stone was cut out of the mountain—yet the cutting of the stone was accomplished without human hands. The stone was flung against the base of the image, causing it to shatter. Then the stone grew and became a mountain that filled the entire earth. The interpretation of this imagery is simplicity itself. The stone is clearly identified for us in Scripture. The apostle Peter writes:

For in Scripture it says:

"See, I lay a stone in Zion,
a chosen and precious cornerstone,
and the one who trusts in him
will never be put to shame."

Now to you who believe, this stone is precious. But to those who do not believe,

> "The stone the builders rejected
>   has become the cornerstone,"

and,

> "A stone that causes people to stumble
>   and a rock that makes them fall."

They stumble because they disobey the message—which is also what they were destined for. (1 Peter 2:6–8)

The Lord Jesus Christ is the Stone that invades human history and strikes at the affairs of humankind. Through Him, God intervenes in history and destroys all the works of human pride and arrogance. The entire structure of civilization crumbles under the impact of this mighty Stone—and the Stone itself grows to fill the entire earth.

This is a vivid depiction of the authority and power of Jesus the Lord—and of His right to rule among the kingdoms of humanity. He is the Stone that God sends to intervene dramatically in human history, demolishing centuries of so-called "human progress." Think of all the human accomplishments that have occurred over the time span covered by King Nebuchadnezzar's dream—from the fabulous Hanging Gardens of Babylon to the Internet, stealth bombers, and interplanetary space probes of the twenty-first century. All of these human accomplishments will come to nothing at the impact of this mighty Stone—and the Stone will grow and expand and fill the entire earth. When this occurs, we will see the beginning of the Lord's millennial kingdom, which was promised by the prophets.

How did King Nebuchadnezzar respond when Daniel interpreted his dream? The closing verses of Daniel 2 reveal the king's response:

> Then King Nebuchadnezzar fell prostrate before Daniel and paid him honor and ordered that an offering and incense be presented to him. The king said to Daniel, "Surely your God is the God of gods and the Lord of kings and a revealer of mysteries, for you were able to reveal this mystery."
>
> Then the king placed Daniel in a high position and lavished many gifts on him. He made him ruler over the entire province of Babylon and placed him in charge of all its wise men. Moreover, at Daniel's request the king appointed Shadrach, Meshach and Abednego administrators over the province of Babylon, while Daniel himself remained at the royal court. (Daniel 2:46–49)

The response of King Nebuchadnezzar should be our response as well. Let us remind ourselves that the God we serve is the Lord who rules over all earthly powers. He is a revealer of mysteries. Let us fall down before Him and give Him honor and make an offering to Him of our daily lives.

AT THE TERMINUS OF CIVILIZATION

What is our part in the grand prophetic scheme of Daniel 2? If we stand (as I believe we do) at the terminus of civilization as we know it, and if we are approaching the end of man's day, as God's prophets have long predicted, then God's kingdom will at last be established—and sooner rather than later. As Peter suggests, it will be our privilege to rejoice in that "chosen and precious cornerstone."

In light of this observation, several questions confront us: What is our relationship to that Stone? Is He the foundation for our lives—or is He coming to destroy all that we have built? Is the return of our Lord an event that thrills us—or threatens us? Will He come as our great Friend—or as a foe?

Although He will destroy all the works of our fallen civilization, your works and mine will stand if we have done them for Christ in obedience to His will. But anything we have done for our own glory will be swept away when that Stone strikes our civilization.

The purpose of biblical prophecy is to remind us to keep our lives balanced. Prophecy is not intended to focus our minds on tomorrow but to focus our minds on what we must do today. You may say, "I can't be focused on God all the time. I've got to make a living." Of course! God wants you to make a living. God's prophetic truth about the future does not relieve us of the need to provide for our families and ourselves.

But His truth reminds us that Jesus is the Lord of our entire lives, including our careers. We can honor God with our weekday work just as surely as we honor Him with our Sunday worship. We can be witnesses in the workplace. We can live out our faith and our Christian values as we encounter customers, clients, coworkers, employees, and employers. We can embody the gospel of Jesus Christ wherever we go, whatever we do.

If we live only to get a paycheck and fatten our retirement account and move up the corporate ladder, we will one day see all of our selfish efforts dispersed upon the winds at the return of Jesus Christ. But if we live to serve Christ in the workplace, in the factory, on the campus, in the barracks, or wherever God has placed us, everything we do will have eternal and lasting significance.

There is a hunger in every human heart to achieve something meaningful and enduring. These great prophetic passages of Scripture are designed to remind us of this all-important question: Am I living as an available instrument for God to use to accomplish His purpose? Am I walking in harmony with His eternal program for history? Or am I achieving only that which will ultimately crumble to dust?

The Stone is coming. That Stone may invade our world sooner than we imagine. Don't fear that invasion. Serve the Lord, welcome His coming invasion, and rejoice when He appears.

4

THE WORLD MENAGERIE

Daniel 7:1–14

The Danish philosopher Søren Kierkegaard recalled a true story with frightening implications. "In a theater," he wrote, "it happened that a fire started offstage. The clown came out to tell the audience. [The people] thought it was a joke and applauded. He told them again, and they became still more hilarious. This is the way, I suppose, that the world will be destroyed—amid the universal hilarity of wits and wags who think it is all a joke."[1]

In our overview of the book of Daniel in chapter 1, we examined the story of Belshazzar in Daniel 5. Belshazzar was the playboy son of the largely uninvolved King Nabonidus, one of the kings who came to the throne a number of years after the death of King Nebuchadnezzar. The pleasure-seeking Belshazzar threw a party in which he, his wives and concubines, and his guests all defiled the gold and silver utensils that had been used for worshiping God in the temple in Jerusalem. Like the theater audience in Kierkegaard's story, these revelers were laughing and applauding even as their doom approached. The nation of Babylon was about to be overthrown, and their souls were about to be judged—yet they were partying and blaspheming as if the end of their world was nothing but a joke.

In the midst of their revelry, a human hand appeared and wrote with its fingers a pronouncement of doom on the wall—and then it was too late. Daniel interpreted the inscription—and within hours, the Persians invaders were inside the walls of Babylon, and Belshazzar and his guests were put to the sword.

But here in Daniel 7, the prophet gives us a flashback to a vision he experienced before the events of Daniel 5. At the time of Daniel's vision, the Babylonian empire was still powerful, and Belshazzar—the last king of Babylon—was in the first year of his reign. The vision described in Daniel 7 occurs about thirty to thirty-five years after King Nebuchadnezzar's dream of the great image, as recorded in Daniel 2. Here, it is Daniel who has the dream, and his dream contains three separate visions.

THE THREE VISIONS OF DANIEL

The first of the three visions is found in Daniel 7:2–6—the vision of the three beasts that arise out of the sea.

The second vision is found in Daniel 7:7–12—the vision of a fourth beast and "the Ancient of Days."

The third vision is found in Daniel 7:13–14—the further vision of the remarkable person called "the Ancient of Days." This vision is an unmistakable appearance of the preincarnate Christ.

In verses 15 through 18, Daniel relates to us a general interpretation of these three visions as told to him by "one of those standing there," undoubtedly an angel.

In verses 19 through 28, the angel focuses on the fourth beast, who is of great significance to us in our own day. The structure of Daniel 7 follows the same general division as Daniel 2, which gave us the dream of King Nebuchadnezzar. Like the image in Nebuchadnezzar's dream, Daniel's vision presents four divisions of history, ending with the invasion of earth by God and the establishment of His kingdom.

In Daniel 2, a great stone was cut out of the mountain, but not by human hands. The stone struck the feet of the image and destroyed the image, symbolizing all the kingdoms of human history. In Daniel 7, the vision of the stone that strikes the image is replaced by a scene in which the Ancient of Days sends the Son of Man to establish His everlasting dominion upon the earth.

Because these two chapters seem to follow the same general pattern, most Bible interpreters view the four beasts of Daniel 7 as depicting the same nations as the four divisions of the dream in Daniel 2: Babylon, Medo-Persia, Greece, and a fourth empire beginning with Rome but extending to the second coming of Jesus Christ. This is called the "historical interpretation" of Daniel 7. According to this view, most of Daniel 7 depicts events that lie in the past, and only the fourth beast concerns us in the present. There are many knowledgeable Bible expositors who support that view, and I have held that view myself in the past.

But I have come to believe that the beasts in Daniel 7 are not historical events, as in Daniel 2. Rather, they are future events. I believe all four of these beasts represent conditions among the nations at a time just prior to the return of Jesus Christ. Daniel's vision, then, presents a kind of "zoom lens" view of the events of the last days.

THE FIRST BEAST

When Daniel relates the first vision, he marks out a specific geographical location where these events will take place:

> In the first year of Belshazzar king of Babylon, Daniel had a dream, and visions passed through his mind as he was lying in bed. He wrote down the substance of his dream.
>
> Daniel said: "In my vision at night I looked, and there before me were the four winds of heaven churning up the great sea. Four great beasts, each different from the others, came up out of the sea.
>
> "The first was like a lion, and it had the wings of an

eagle. I watched until its wings were torn off and it was lifted from the ground so that it stood on two feet like a human being, and the mind of a human was given to it.

"And there before me was a second beast, which looked like a bear. It was raised up on one of its sides, and it had three ribs in its mouth between its teeth. It was told, 'Get up and eat your fill of flesh!'

"After that, I looked, and there before me was another beast, one that looked like a leopard. And on its back it had four wings like those of a bird. This beast had four heads, and it was given authority to rule." (Daniel 7:1–6)

When Scripture speaks of "the sea," it refers to the Mediterranean Sea. The Mediterranean Sea forms the western boundary of Israel. Daniel saw the four winds of heaven blowing upon and churning up the great sea. The locale of these visions is the Mediterranean, and this vision describes an epic struggle for mastery of the Mediterranean region.

Four distinct beasts rise up out of the sea. Daniel's description makes it clear that these four beasts symbolize four nations. I think it's significant that these nations are depicted as beasts, not as parts of a man, as in Nebuchadnezzar's dream in Daniel 2. The reason these nations are depicted as beasts is because this dream represents God's view of the nations.

In Daniel 2, we are presented with a dream from Nebuchadnezzar's point of view. The nations were depicted as Nebuchadnezzar would see them, symbolized by their outward glory. Gold and silver spoke of the glory of fabulous wealth of the Babylonians and Persians. Bronze, a metal widely used for armor and weaponry, spoke of the military might of Greece. And iron symbolized the unbreakable, iron-fisted rule of Rome.

But from God's view, there is nothing glorious about these nations. They battled each other with the ferocity of the unreasoning brutes. That's why, here in Daniel 7, the nations are depicted as animals. You can hear these creatures growling, snarling, and snapping at one another as you read Daniel's account. And if you set Daniel's vision aside and read your newspaper or watch a session of the United Nations on television, you'll hear the same kind of bestial growling, snarling, and snapping.

The first beast is described as a lion-like creature with an eagle's wings. As Daniel watches, the wings are torn off, and the creature is made to stand on two feet and think like a human being. What should we make of this strange beast? According to the historical view, this creature symbolizes Babylon, the nation in which Daniel lived at the time. But some features of this vision would indicate that this is not the correct interpretation.

First, the date of the vision contradicts this interpretation. The vision occurred in the first year of Belshazzar, the last king of Babylon. Yet Daniel sees the beast coming up out of the sea, which strongly indicates a future event. Historically, Babylon had long been established. The lion-like creature that emerges from the sea suggests a nation that had not yet emerged onto the scene.

Second, most of the book of Daniel is written in Hebrew, but the section from Daniel chapters 2 through 7 is written in a closely related language, Aramaic. Hebrew and Aramaic are sufficiently similar that Hebrew and Aramaic speakers could largely understand each other, much as Swedish and Norwegian speakers can. Aramaic is the language Jesus spoke during his earthly ministry, and the visions in Daniel 2 and 7 are probably told in Aramaic because they both pertain to the Gentile nations and not to the Jews.

I think it's unlikely that chapter 7 would simply repeat the message of chapter 2—especially since this entire Aramaic section is probably addressed to the same audience. So it seems to me that the fact that this entire section is written in Aramaic further suggests that Daniel's vision in chapter 7 is subject to a different interpretation than King Nebuchadnezzar's vision in chapter 2.

Third, there is nothing in the history of Babylon that clearly corresponds to the description of the first beast. The most common interpretation of the first beast is that it refers to King Nebuchadnezzar's period of madness, as recorded in Daniel 4. In accordance with Daniel's prophecy, the king went insane and ate grass like an animal for seven years—God's judgment on Nebuchadnezzar because of the pride of his heart. At the end of the seven years, King Nebuchadnezzar was cured of his insanity and restored to his throne. So, according to this interpretation, when the wings are torn off of the beast and it is made to stand and a human mind is given to it, that is a reference to Nebuchadnezzar being restored from his insanity.

The biggest problem with this theory is that the insanity and restoration of King Nebuchadnezzar took place at least twenty years before Daniel received this vision. It seems highly unlikely that God would give Daniel a prophetic vision referring to past events.

Instead, the vision of the first beast seems to symbolize a mysterious decline in the power of a nation that seeks mastery over the Mediterranean region. The decline of power is represented by the wings being plucked off the beast; the nation then transitions from the pursuit of military might to more intellectual or moral pursuits.

As I pondered this first beast, I was struck by a remarkable parallel between this beast and the British Empire since World War II. I don't claim that this beast definitely represents Great Britain, but I do see strong parallels. The British Empire has long been symbolized by a lion. Wings are a symbol of speed and power. In this vision, however, the wings are torn off, which indicates that the lion has been stripped of much of its power—much as Great Britain has lost much of its empire. Though Great Britain has continued to assert its military power in regions such as the Falklands and in the twenty-first-century wars in Iraq and Afghanistan, Britain is clearly not the globe-spanning military power it once was. Yet the tiny island nation continues to assert a strong cultural influence on the world.

I was astonished when I first read a book called *The Coming Prince* by Sir Robert Anderson, originally published in 1881. For many years during the reign of Queen Victoria, Anderson was the head of Scotland Yard in London. He was an avid student of Scripture who applied his keen investigative skills to the various mysteries of Bible prophecy. In his book, he makes this amazing statement:

> May not the opening portion of this vision then refer to the gigantic struggle [that] must come some day for supremacy in the Mediterranean, which will doubtless carry with it the sovereignty of the world? The lion may possibly typify England, whose vast naval power may be symbolized by the eagles' wings. The plucking of the wings may represent the loss of her position as mistress of the seas.[2]

Why is that statement so astonishing? It's because, when Anderson wrote those words, England was at the zenith of her power as a maritime nation. In the days of Queen Victoria, the British fleet dominated the oceans of the world. It is hard to imagine how Sir Robert Anderson could have foreseen the current decline of Great Britain's military power and her transition into a nation characterized more by moral and intellectual influence than military might. The fact that Anderson read this prophecy and foresaw Britain's decline as a military power is nothing less than amazing.

THE SECOND BEAST

Let's continue on and see if the second beast fits any known nation in our world today. Daniel tells us that the second beast was like a bear. And it reared up, showing three animal ribs in its mouth between its teeth. Then a voice said to the bear-like beast, "Get up and eat your fill of flesh!"

According to the historical view, this bear-like beast is a symbol of the Medo-Persian Empire, which followed Babylon on the historical scene. But there are major problems with this view. For example, in Daniel 8, we see that the Medo-Persian Empire is specifically named, and it is symbolized there in the form of the great two-horned ram, not a bear. It seems unlikely that Scripture would create confusion by employing two symbolic animals to represent the same empire.

Also, in Daniel's vision, the bear-like creature is said to be "raised up on one of its sides" (7:5). Those who take the historical view suggest that this detail refers to the division between the Medes and the Persians, with the Persians being dominant. But some Hebrew scholars tell us that "raised up on one of its sides" is a mistranslation. What Daniel is really saying about the bear is that "it made for itself one dominion." That is likely a more accurate translation of the Aramaic.

If the bear-like creature refers to a nation that is in existence prior to the return of the Lord Jesus, then we have to conclude that it is more likely that this creature symbolizes Russia. After the fall of the Soviet Union (USSR) in 1991, the government of the Russian Federation continued to rule a nation spanning nine time zones, from the Baltic Sea in the west to the Bering Strait in the east. Whether the government of Russia was czarist or communist or a republic as it is today, Russia has long been militant, aggressive, and domineering. In both its Soviet and post-Soviet versions, Russia has sought to project its power into the Middle East and to acquire Mediterranean supremacy.

The image of the bear-like beast with three ribs in its mouth, eating its fill of flesh, reminds us of the bloody history of the Russian (or Soviet) nation. The bear gorged itself on flesh during the Stalin years, as tens of millions of people died in the Russian and Ukrainian famines of 1932–1933 (caused by deliberate government policies), or in the Soviet purges, executions, ethnic deportations, religious persecutions, terror campaigns, and gulags. The Russian/Soviet nation has also eaten much flesh by dominating and oppressing numerous client states, from the Warsaw Pact nations to Cuba, Angola, Mozambique, Afghanistan, North Korea, and Vietnam.

It's significant that the Russian/Soviet nation has long been symbolized as a brutal bear. Books and plays have depicted Russia as a bear since the 1600s, and the Soviet Union itself adopted the bear motif for the 1980 Moscow Olympics—though it tried to make the Russian bear seem cuddly and cute with its Misha teddy bear mascot. The truest representation of the Russian bear is that of Daniel 7:5—the raging, bellowing bear-like creature crunching three ribs between its mouth, making for itself one dominion.

Is it significant that the bear-like beast is shown munching on three ribs? Do the three ribs suggest three specific nations? I don't know. Perhaps the identity of those three "ribs" will become apparent in the time shortly before the Lord returns.

THE MYSTERIOUS THIRD BEAST

Daniel describes a third beast in verse 6—a beast that "looked like a leopard. And on its back it had four wings like those of a bird. This beast had four heads, and it was given authority to rule." According to the historical view, this beast would represent Greece, the kingdom of Alexander the Great. But again, if we turn to Daniel 8, we see Greece clearly depicted as a male goat with a large horn between his eyes.

Proponents of the historical view suggest that the four heads of the leopard-like beast refer to the fact that, following the death of Alexander, his kingdom was divided among his four generals. This is historically true. The problem with this view is that this beast is depicted as having four heads from its very beginning. We will see a clear depiction of the four divisions of Alexander's kingdom in Daniel 8. But here, in Daniel 7, the four-headed beast appears to be engaged from the beginning in a struggle for mastery of the Mediterranean region.

The four wings suggest the ability to move quickly and strike without warning, much as Israel did during the Six-Day War in 1967. But Israel does not seek to dominate its Mediterranean neighbors. It seeks only to defend itself against hostile neighbors. The identity of this four-headed leopard-like beast may not be visible to us as yet. Perhaps its identity will become clear in the days shortly before the Lord's return.

At any rate, it is clear that the first three beasts represent three great nations that struggle for mastery of the Mediterranean region. Although they are described one after another, it is likely that they will all appear at the same time, vying with each other and struggling for control of the great sea and its surrounding lands.

THE FOURTH BEAST

Next, Daniel relates his second vision, and a terrible fourth beast comes into view. The rest of Daniel 7 focuses on this horrific symbol:

> "After that, in my vision at night I looked, and there before me was a fourth beast—terrifying and frightening and very powerful. It had large iron teeth; it crushed and devoured its victims and trampled underfoot whatever was left. It was different from all the former beasts, and it had ten horns.
>
> "While I was thinking about the horns, there before me was another horn, a little one, which came up among them; and three of the first horns were uprooted before it. This horn had eyes like the eyes of a human being and a mouth that spoke boastfully." (Daniel 7:7–8)

The fourth beast and its symbolic meaning form the central theme of the chapter. Several noteworthy features of this beast are readily apparent:

First, Daniel tells us that this beast had great iron teeth. The reference to iron suggests a connection to the iron kingdom of Daniel 2, which is the fourth empire to occupy leadership in the affairs of the world. The fourth empire began with the Roman Empire, which was marked by an iron-fisted rule.

Second, this beast is described as shattering all opposition and trampling it underfoot. This is markedly similar to a description of the iron kingdom in Daniel 2, which suggests that the fourth beast conquers the first three beasts and takes over their power.

Third, the beast is described as having ten horns—then an eleventh horn, a little one, appears. Next, three of the first ten horns are torn out by the roots. It may be that the three horns are identical to the first three beasts. The removal of the three horns may suggest that the first three beasts that appeared in the first vision are ultimately subdued and conquered by the fourth beast.

Fourth, the ten horns of the fourth beast seem to correspond to the ten toes of the image in Daniel 2. You may remember a cryptic statement in Daniel 2:44: "In the time of those kings, the God of heaven will set up a kingdom that will never be destroyed, nor will it be left to another people. It will crush all those kingdoms and bring them to an end, but it will itself endure forever." The reason this statement is cryptic is that there is no other reference to "those kings" in Daniel 2. The prophet Daniel had referred to kingdoms, but not to kings. The reference to kings seems to come out of nowhere.

Now, in Daniel 7, we see a beast with ten horns, and it is clearly a coalition of ten nations that unite together to give their power to one king or nation. An eleventh horn, a little one, joins later, overpowers three of the original ten horns (which may represent the three beasts of the previous vision), and becomes the dominant power on the earth. It makes its appearance by joining the struggle for Mediterranean mastery.

INSIGHT FROM REVELATION

The book of Revelation sheds further light on this fourth beast in Daniel 7. One of the most remarkable features of the Bible is the way the various prophetic passages fit together like pieces of a jigsaw puzzle, even though those passages may have been written centuries apart. In this case, the book of Daniel and the book of Revelation are separated by some six hundred years, yet the parallels between these two books are truly remarkable. In Revelation, the apostle John writes:

> And I saw a beast coming out of the sea. It had ten horns and seven heads, with ten crowns on its horns, and on each head a blasphemous name. The beast I saw resembled a leopard, but had feet like those of a bear and a mouth like that of a lion. (Revelation 13:1–2)

Do you see the similarity? The beast John describes in Revelation features characteristics of the first three beasts in Daniel 7—the lion, the bear, and the leopard—and they appear as features of the great beast that John sees in his vision. This description suggests once more that, in some way, Daniel's fourth beast seems to conquer and combine the other three beasts into a single super-powerful entity.

In Revelation 17, John presents another scene that helps us to interpret the vision of the fourth beast in the book of Daniel:

> One of the seven angels who had the seven bowls came and said to me, "Come, I will show you the punishment of the great prostitute, who sits by many waters. With her the kings of the earth committed adultery, and the inhabitants of the earth were intoxicated with the wine of her adulteries."
>
> Then the angel carried me away in the Spirit into a wilderness. There I saw a woman sitting on a scarlet beast that was covered with blasphemous names and had seven heads and ten horns. (Revelation 17:1–3)

The symbolism here is remarkable. This great prostitute stands for the false church—not a church of any particular denomination or sect, but all false religion and pseudo-Christianity. The prostitute is seated first upon many waters. Then, when John gets a closer view, he sees her seated upon a beast with seven heads and ten horns. The waters, therefore, symbolize the same reality the beast symbolizes. John relates to us the interpretation of the waters:

> And the angel said to me, "The waters that you saw, where the prostitute is seated, are peoples and multitudes and nations and languages." (Revelation 17:15 ESV)

Multitudes of peoples of many nations will join together, representing many languages. All of this agrees with the vision Daniel has shown us—that the fourth kingdom, the fourth beast of chapter 7, is made up of many nations, a Western empire joining together in a great confederacy to act as a unit. It is made up of peoples and multitudes and nations and languages, yet in its final form it is headed up by ten kings or kingdoms that unite together:

> "The ten horns you saw are ten kings who have not yet received a kingdom, but who for one hour will receive authority as kings along with the beast. They have one purpose and will give their power and authority to the beast. They will wage war against the Lamb, but the Lamb will triumph over them because he is Lord of lords and King of kings—and with him will be his called, chosen and faithful followers." (Revelation 17:12–14)

John gives us a clear indication of the time in which these events will occur. This ten-nation confederacy arises immediately before the return of Jesus Christ, who is the Lamb who conquers the nations of the earth.

THE ANCIENT OF DAYS

Turning back to Daniel 7, we examine the next part of Daniel's vision—the appearance of the Ancient of Days:

"As I looked,

> "thrones were set in place,
>> and the Ancient of Days took his seat.
> His clothing was as white as snow;
>> the hair of his head was white like wool.
> His throne was flaming with fire,
>> and its wheels were all ablaze.
> A river of fire was flowing,
>> coming out from before him.
> Thousands upon thousands attended him;
>> ten thousand times ten thousand stood before
>> him.
> The court was seated,
>> and the books were opened.

"Then I continued to watch because of the boastful words the horn was speaking. I kept looking until the beast was slain and its body destroyed and thrown into the blazing fire. (The other beasts had been stripped of their authority, but were allowed to live for a period of time.)" (Daniel 7:9–12)

This vision of the Ancient of Days is similar to the vision John records in Revelation 4 and 5 in which the apostle looks into heaven and beholds a judgment scene with God upon a throne and twenty-four elders on thrones around Him. They too were passing judgment on the affairs of earth, just as Daniel sees taking place here, with countless angels waiting upon God's word. God is in the midst of His council, and as the council debates the matters of earth, sentence is passed upon the blasphemous horn, the last ruler of the fourth kingdom—this horn that had "eyes like the eyes of a human being and a mouth that spoke boastfully." We will see more of him in our next study on the latter half of Daniel 7.

THE DOMINION OF THE SON OF MAN

The next vision Daniel witnesses is a vision of the One who is chosen to execute the judgment of the Ancient of Days:

> "In my vision at night I looked, and there before me was one like a son of man, coming with the clouds of heaven. He approached the Ancient of Days and was led into his presence. He was given authority, glory and sovereign power; all nations and peoples of every language worshiped him. His dominion is an everlasting dominion that will not pass away, and his kingdom is one that will never be destroyed." (Daniel 7:13–14)

Who is this "one like a son of man"? Who else could it be but Jesus the Lord, the promised Messiah? It is the same Person we see in Revelation 1:

> I turned around to see the voice that was speaking to me. And when I turned I saw seven golden lampstands, and among the lampstands was someone like a son of man, dressed in a robe reaching down to his feet and with a golden sash around his chest. The hair on his head was white like wool, as white as snow, and his eyes were like blazing fire. His feet were like bronze glowing in a furnace, and his voice was like the sound of rushing waters. In his right hand he held seven stars, and coming out of his mouth was a sharp, double-edged sword. His face was like the sun shining in all its brilliance.
>
> When I saw him, I fell at his feet as though dead. Then he placed his right hand on me and said: "Do not be afraid. I am the First and the Last. I am the Living One; I was dead, and now look, I am alive for ever and ever! And I hold the keys of death and Hades." (Revelation 1:12–18)

He is the One who possesses all power in heaven and on earth. He holds the keys of death and Hades, and He alone is worthy to open the seven-sealed book:

> Then I saw a Lamb, looking as if it had been slain, standing at the center of the throne, encircled by the four living creatures and the elders. The Lamb had seven horns and seven eyes, which are the seven spirits of God sent out into all the earth. He went and took the scroll from the right hand of him who sat on the throne. And when he had taken it, the four living creatures and the twenty-four elders fell down before the Lamb. Each one had a harp and they were holding golden bowls full of incense, which are the prayers of God's people. And they sang a new song, saying:
>
> "You are worthy to take the scroll
>   and to open its seals,
> because you were slain,
>   and with your blood you purchased for God
>   persons from every tribe and language and
>   people and nation." (Revelation 5:6–9)

In Daniel 7, the Lord Jesus (called "one like a son of man," v. 13) comes with the clouds of heaven to stand before the Ancient of Days, who is God the Father. And the Ancient of Days gives to the Son "authority, glory and sovereign power; all nations and peoples of every language worshiped him. His dominion is an everlasting dominion that will not pass away" (v. 14). This passage in Daniel was probably on the Lord's mind when He addressed the chief priests who had arrested Him and charged Him with blasphemy. He told them, "But I tell you, from now on you will see the Son of Man seated at the right hand of Power and coming on the clouds of heaven" (Matthew 26:64 ESV).

What should we make of all the wars, terrors, and catastrophes that precede the return of Jesus Christ? Clearly, God is allowing sinful humanity to run its course until all the evil pretensions of the human heart are exposed. When history reaches its lowest ebb, when the human sin breaks forth in all its most vile and brutal forms, then God will intervene. That is the central teaching of the Word of God, and it is taught by the prophets of old, who spoke under the inspiration of the Holy Spirit. It is also taught by the New Testament apostles and by the Lord Jesus Christ. The Lord quotes the book of Daniel and gives us the same picture Daniel gives concerning His return: "When the Son of Man comes in his glory, and all the angels with him, he will sit on his glorious throne," (Matthew 25:31 TNIV). Then His throne will be established and all nations shall gather before Him. (The Lord gives us this same picture in Matthew 24 and 25.)

This is the outline of history as given to us by Daniel, the book of Revelation, and the Lord Jesus himself. If this prophetic outline is not true, then Christianity is a fraud. God tells us that He intends to fulfill these prophetic visions exactly as He has described them in His Word.

THE MENAGERIE UNLEASHED

What does all of this mean to you as an individual? What does it mean that God will not permit the human race to work out its problems? The secular world is always trying to solve human problems through new educational approaches, new political or economic theories, new social programs, more and stricter laws, and on and on—but these "solutions" only seemed to make the human condition worse than ever before. The solutions we seek for crime, child abuse, poverty, unemployment, overpopulation, terrorism, and war are always beyond our reach. Again and again throughout history, we have shown that humanity lacks the capacity to work out its own problems.

The human race repeatedly rejects God's solution to human sin and suffering. So God, who has given the human race free will—including the freedom to reject Him and His Son Jesus—allows the human race to go its own way and sink deeper and deeper into its self-made morass. God permits the human race to demonstrate its own futility and helplessness. That is the teaching of Bible prophecy.

In our own time, we are witnessing various struggles that remind us of the images in Daniel's visions. We are seeing nations struggling for supremacy over the Mediterranean region. Every expert in the field of geopolitics has a watchful eye on that region. There is unrest across North Africa, from Morocco to Egypt. Saudi Arabia seeks to control events in the region by wielding oil as a weapon. Palestinians continually harass the Israelis with random acts of terror and rocket attacks. Iraq, the land once known as Babylonia, the land of Daniel's captivity, continues to be an unstable and violent nation. The nations of Syria and Lebanon also remain dangerously unstable and violent. Iran, once known as Persia, continually breathes threats, continuing its pursuit of nuclear weapons while promising to wipe Israel off the map.

The region around the Mediterranean is the crossroads of history. It has always been so, and it will continue to be so until the Lord returns to bring human history to a close. We wonder if the events we witness on the nightly news are laying the groundwork for the fulfillment of Daniel's vision and the unleashing of this strange prophetic menagerie upon the world. Will the symbolic beasts of Daniel's vision soon stride the earth in the form of nations and armies, clashing and battling each other for supremacy? Will the events that are foretold in Daniel's vision be fulfilled tomorrow? Next year? Centuries from now? God alone knows.

I can't say with any certainty that the fulfillment of these prophecies is just around the corner. But I can say that events are clearly moving in that direction. Events we see today seem to be leading toward the final clash of prophetic beasts that are pictured here. We don't know God's timetable, but we can be confident that as the story unfolds it will follow the pattern that Daniel, Revelation, the other prophets and apostles, and Jesus himself, have outlined for us.

Our sovereign God is in control of history. As we consider the part each of us plays in human history, we must ask, "Am I on the right side of history? Am I investing my life in the things that will last for all eternity? Am I using my influence to reach others for Jesus Christ? Am I redeeming the time that remains to me in these evil days? Am I allowing God to use me as His chosen instrument in this fallen and dying world?"

Even though the world seems to be spinning out of control, God is always in control. As we face these great prophetic revelations, may God give us the faith to trust Him, to obey Him, and to live confidently as faithful servants of the Lord of history.

5

THE COMING CAESAR
Daniel 7:15–28

One of the most enduring guessing games in Christian history is the game of "Name the Antichrist." Many Christians in the first century AD were convinced that one of the brutal Roman Caesars, such as Caligula or Nero, had to be the Antichrist. The worldly power and personal debaucheries of these tyrants, plus their cruel and bloodthirsty persecution of the Christian church, made them ideal candidates for the role.

As centuries passed and the Catholic Church became a powerful political institution, various popes (especially the flagrantly corrupt popes such as Gregory IX in the thirteenth century or Leo X during the Protestant Reformation) were suspected of being the Antichrist. During the seventeenth century, the Old Believers sect that separated from the Russian Orthodox Church believed that the Russian czar, Peter the Great, had to be the Antichrist.

In more recent times, we have seen other political figures identified as the Antichrist, from Hitler and Mussolini during World War II to Henry Kissinger and Mikhail Gorbachev in the Cold War era. You have also probably heard speculation that this or that American president had to be the Antichrist. Whenever believers suffer persecution or witness cataclysmic world events, there is a tendency to identify a hated, feared religious or political leader as the Antichrist of Bible prophecy.

The rise of this evil, world-dominating figure, the Antichrist, is predicted throughout the prophetic passages of Scripture, in both the Old Testament and the New. He is even foretold by Jesus himself. He will be a cruel, despotic leader with Caesar-like arrogance and pretension, and he will dominate world events shortly before the Lord's return.

All the prophetic passages of Daniel that we have examined so far have been leading to the revelation of this strange and sinister being, the Antichrist. We come to that revelation here in the last half of Daniel 7. This section falls into three natural divisions:

Daniel 7:15–18: A general interpretation of the strange beasts of Daniel's vision.

Daniel 7:19–22: A review of the facts regarding the fourth beast.

Daniel 7:23–28: A specialized interpretation of the fourth beast.

JESUS IN THE OLD TESTAMENT

Let's begin by examining the first division:

> "I, Daniel, was troubled in spirit, and the visions that passed through my mind disturbed me. I approached one of those standing there and asked him the meaning of all this.
>
> "So he told me and gave me the interpretation of these things: 'The four great beasts are four kings that will rise from the earth. But the holy people of the Most High will receive the kingdom and will possess it forever—yes, for ever and ever.'" (Daniel 7:15–18)

Here, for the first time in Daniel 7, we learn the personal reaction of the prophet to this strange series of night visions. He is understandably alarmed and puzzled by all he has seen. He knows that these visions portend tremendous future events, but he doesn't know how soon they are scheduled to occur, and he is puzzled as to their meaning. We learn here of the presence of an interpreting angel, and Daniel asks this angel the meaning of his visions.

Later, in Daniel 9, we discover the identity of this interpreting angel. Daniel tells us he is Gabriel, the same angel God later sent to announce the birth of Jesus to both Joseph and Mary, as recorded in the opening chapters of Matthew and Luke. Gabriel seems to serve a special role as the announcer and interpreter of major events on God's calendar. Gabriel appears to the prophet Daniel and interprets the visions.

Gabriel highlights two elements in this strange vision of the four beasts arising out of the sea. One is that the four beasts are "four kings that will rise from the earth" (7:17). The wording makes it clear that the historical interpretation of this passage, which links Daniel's vision to the historical rise of Babylon, followed by Medo-Persia, then Greece, then Rome, cannot be accurate. The angel says that the beasts represent future events, not historical events.

We know from the first verse of chapter 7 that Daniel saw this vision shortly before the end of the Babylonian Empire, during "the first year of Belshazzar," Babylon's last king. The first beast represented the future rise of a kingdom—yet Babylon had not only risen, but it had also ruled world events for centuries and was then approaching its ultimate collapse and defeat. These facts help us to confirm that Daniel's vision depicts four great nations that occupy the Mediterranean region shortly before the return of Jesus Christ. This vision depicts the closing days of Gentile rule.

The second element the angel Gabriel highlights for Daniel is that the ultimate end of these cataclysmic events is the establishment of the long-promised kingdom of God. History does not end in destruction. It continues on to reconstruction. This final kingdom was decreed by the Ancient of Days (God). In Daniel 7:13–14, we saw that the Ancient of Days grants dominion over the entire world to "one like a son of man" who arrived among "the clouds of heaven." This is an unmistakable Old Testament reference to the Lord Jesus Christ.

In Daniel 7:18, we learn that not only will "one like a son of man" possess dominion, but also "the holy people of the Most High will receive the kingdom and will possess it forever—yes, for ever and ever." This is a new revelation from Gabriel; the fact that God's "holy people" will also take part in possessing the kingdom was not mentioned in Daniel's description of his vision. God's holy people do not take possession of the kingdom by any act of their own. Instead, we see that Jesus ("one like a son of man") takes possession of the kingdom from God the Most High, and Jesus in turn gives the kingdom to God's holy people as a free and unearned gift of grace. Thus, God's holy people join the Lord Jesus in ruling over the earth.

WAR AGAINST GOD'S HOLY PEOPLE

Following this introduction, we come to the fourth beast—the strange ten-horned creature that is the fourth of the series of beasts Daniel saw rising out of the sea. We need to pay special attention to the eleventh horn that rises up after the first ten horns. Daniel asks Gabriel concerning this beast:

> "Then I wanted to know the meaning of the fourth beast, which was different from all the others and most terrifying, with its iron teeth and bronze claws—the beast that crushed and devoured its victims and trampled underfoot whatever was left. I also wanted to know about the ten horns on its head and about the other horn that came up, before which three of them fell—the horn that looked more imposing than the others and that had eyes and a mouth that spoke boastfully. As I watched, this horn was waging war against the holy people and defeating them, until the Ancient of Days came and pronounced

judgment in favor of the holy people of the Most High, and the time came when they possessed the kingdom." (Daniel 7:19–22)

Most of what Gabriel tells us in these verses is essentially the same as what we previously saw in Daniel 7:7–8: the beast with the iron teeth that crushed, trampled, and devoured its victims; ten horns, three of which were later removed; and so forth. But Gabriel provides one detail that we haven't seen before. He tells us of the horn that grew up, waged war against God's holy people, and was prevailing against them until the Ancient of Days—the Most High God himself—arrived, pronounced judgment, and ended the war.

This scene was not included in Daniel's earlier description of his vision. We learn from Gabriel that when these four nations rise up together, it will be a time of intense religious persecution, a time of war against God's saints—and the beast will prevail against God's people for a time. The description of events in these verses undoubtedly connects with the Lord's words in Matthew 24, when He told His disciples on the Mount of Olives, just before His crucifixion:

> "Then you will be handed over to be persecuted and put to death, and you will be hated by all nations because of me. At that time many will turn away from the faith and will betray and hate each other, and many false prophets will appear and deceive many people. Because of the increase of wickedness, the love of most will grow cold, but the one who stands firm to the end will be saved. And this gospel of the kingdom will be preached in the whole world as a testimony to all nations, and then the end will come." (Matthew 24:9–14)

The events described by the angel Gabriel in Daniel 7 are confirmed to us and reemphasized by the Lord Jesus himself.

THE BEAST THAT DEVOURED THE WHOLE EARTH

Continuing with the angel Gabriel's interpretation, we come to the closing section of Daniel 7, where Gabriel answers Daniel's inquiry regarding the fourth beast. The angel offers a detailed explanation of what the strange symbolism means, especially the symbolism of the little horn. Each verse of this section covers one stage of interpretation, so let's examine this passage verse by verse:

> "He gave me this explanation: 'The fourth beast is a fourth kingdom that will appear on earth. It will be different from all the other kingdoms and will devour the whole earth, trampling it down and crushing it.'" (Daniel 7:23)

This interpretation builds upon what we have already learned. Gabriel summarizes the strange course of the iron rule of Roman sovereignty over the earth. The fourth kingdom began with the Roman Empire, but (as the angel said to Daniel) the fourth kingdom would be different from all other kingdoms that went before. It is different because it is not a single nation, but a collection of nations. It is, in fact, all of Western civilization. It is this collective nature that marks the fourth kingdom as unique in human history.

Revelation 17 similarly describes a beast that is made up of a number of nations and tongues and kingdoms. Unlike many nations today that are held together by ethnicity or language or geography, the fourth kingdom will be comprised of many peoples, languages, and regions. It will be bound together and will dominate the world by a philosophical force and cultural heritage that transcends language and boundaries.

Consider these questions: Why have Western languages dominated world trade for the past two thousand years? In the time of Christ, the dominant languages were Greek (largely because of the conquests of Alexander the Great) and Latin (the language of Rome). After the fall of Rome, the dominant languages were Neo-Latin languages descended from Latin, such as Spanish, Portuguese, and

French. English, which is spoken all over the world as the language of commerce and diplomacy, was originally a Germanic language, but the Norman conquest of England in the eleventh century infused English with borrowings from the Neo-Latin Norman-French tongue. So the dominant languages have descended from the Roman Empire.

Why has Western dress become the standard around the world in our own day? Even in Asia, India, Africa, and other parts of the non-Western world, you see Western modes of fashion, from women's dresses and men's business suits to blue jeans and athletic shoes. The same can be said of Western technology, Western forms of entertainment (from movies to pop music), and Western cultural expressions (including art and symphonic music). Western-style democracies have proliferated throughout the world, and Western-style cities—replete with skyscrapers, traffic congestion, crime, noise, and pollution—have also become a global phenomenon.

Gabriel said that this fourth kingdom would "be different from all the other kingdoms and will devour the whole earth, trampling it down and crushing it" (Daniel 7:23). At first glance, this seems to be a reference to a mighty militaristic power that imposes death, destruction, and totalitarian government on the world. However, this description might also be applied to our own Western culture, which has devoured the earth, trampled it down, and crushed it through the weight of its own political, commercial, cultural, and technological influence. There is no denying that Western civilization, descended largely from the Roman Empire, has had a strange, powerful, and impressive impact on the world.

THE COMING CAESAR

The angel Gabriel goes on to tell Daniel:

> "The ten horns are ten kings who will come from this king-dom. After them another king will arise, different from the earlier ones; he will subdue three kings." (Daniel 7:24)

Here we have the final form of the fourth kingdom. Two great political changes must occur before the return of Jesus Christ in glory: (1) the restoration of the Jewish people to the Promised Land, Palestine, which was predicted for centuries and has now been fulfilled; and (2) the tenfold division of the Roman earth. We see this condition emphasized in several passages of Scripture, indicating that this change must occur before the return of Jesus Christ.

The tenfold division of the fourth kingdom develops gradually after it first appears. First, there are ten kings who share power together in a confederation. Then an eleventh "horn" arises—an entity that is initially small and unpretentious. Soon, three of the first ten kings are overthrown or incorporated by the eleventh "horn." Finally, all ten unite in giving their power and authority to the eleventh, the "little horn" that is mentioned here.

You cannot read this account without seeing that this "little horn" is an individual, not a nation. As Daniel described him in verse 8, "This horn had eyes like the eyes of a human being and a mouth that spoke boastfully." He is the final and greatest Caesar of the fourth kingdom. The Roman Empire began with a series of Caesars who established a norm for dictatorship throughout all of human history. They symbolize the supreme power of the state vested in a single individual. The "little horn" mentioned here will be the coming and final Caesar of the world.

The angel Gabriel goes on to tell us about this coming Caesar:

> "He will speak against the Most High and oppress his
> holy people and try to change the set times and the laws.
> The holy people will be delivered into his hands for a
> time, times and half a time." (Daniel 7:25)

Here is new information that we did not have before. There are four distinct and recognizable elements that Gabriel discloses to us regarding this strange and powerful being:

First, he blasphemes and opposes God—he "will speak against the Most High." In other passages of Scripture, we see that this individual did not begin his career as a blasphemer. After gaining power, he begins to blaspheme God.

Second, he persecutes and oppresses God's holy people and makes war against them. He afflicts the saints physically and mentally. It is likely that this individual will use brainwashing, drugs, and torture techniques to produce mental exhaustion, terror, and compliance, with the ultimate goal of turning believers away from faith in God.

Third, he will "try to change the set times and the laws." The meaning of the statement is obscure, but it's possible that it refers to an attempt to revise the calendar and abolish God's law. Today, we date all events from *Anno Domini*, "the year of our Lord." Every time we write the current date and year on any document, we acknowledge the birth of Christ. This future Caesar may be so hostile to Jesus Christ that he will attempt to eliminate all reference to Christ as the hinge of history.

He will try to change the law—perhaps a reference to the constitutions by which nations are governed, or a reference to natural law, the fundamental laws of society, economics, and human relations. He is a supremely arrogant individual who considers himself the new incarnation of all that people believe about God—and thus he feels he has the right to alter fundamental and basic law.

Fourth, though he will reach the pinnacle of power, the time of his power is limited. We read, "The holy people will be delivered into his hands for a time, times and half a time." Elsewhere in Daniel we see what is meant by "a time." Nebuchadnezzar, in Daniel 4, was afflicted with insanity for "seven times," meaning seven years. So a "time" is a year. If we take a time, two times, and half a time, and add them together we have three and a half years. This timing agrees precisely with predictions elsewhere in Scripture that limit the time of Antichrist's power to twelve hundred and sixty days or forty-two months (both of which equal three and a half years—see Daniel 12:7 and Revelation 11:2–3; 12:6, 14; and 13:5).

The parallelism between Daniel and Revelation is striking. In Revelation 13 we see that the strange beast that John saw rising up out of the sea closely parallels the beast Daniel describes. John wrote:

> And I saw a beast coming out of the sea. It had ten horns and seven heads, with ten crowns on its horns, and on each head a blasphemous name. The beast I saw resembled a leopard, but had feet like those of a bear and a mouth like that of a lion. (Revelation 13:1–2)

John's beast embodies all the characteristics of the first three beasts of Daniel's vision. And John goes on to say:

> The beast was given a mouth to utter proud words and blasphemies and to exercise its authority for forty-two months. (Revelation 13:5)

Notice how clearly this description of the beast accords with what Daniel says about the horn that had "eyes like the eyes of a human being and a mouth that spoke boastfully" (7:8) and who "will speak against the Most High" (v. 25). In Revelation we learn that this individual will "utter proud words and blasphemies," and he will be allowed by God to exercise authority for forty-two months—that is, for three and a half years. The description of this individual in Revelation continues:

> It was given power to wage war against God's holy people and to conquer them. And it was given authority over every tribe, people, language and nation. All inhabitants of the earth will worship the beast—all whose names have not been written in the Lamb's book of life, the Lamb who was slain from the creation of the world. (Revelation 13:7–8)

Clearly, we have an exact parallel between the little horn of Daniel 7 and the beast of Revelation 13. Turning back to Daniel 7, we read of the doom of this individual:

> "'But the court will sit, and his power will be taken away and completely destroyed forever. Then the sovereignty, power and greatness of all the kingdoms under heaven will be handed over to the holy people of the Most High. His kingdom will be an everlasting kingdom, and all rulers will worship and obey him.'" (Daniel 7:26–27)

When the angel tells Daniel that the court will sit in judgment, this means that the heavenly council will pass sentence upon this blasphemous and God-defying man, the last Caesar.

THE COMING COLLAPSE

It's encouraging to see that man's evil is always limited. Evil men can only go so far—then they bump up against the time limit that God has set for them. Paul gives us further details regarding this man in 2 Thessalonians 2:7:

> For the secret power of lawlessness is already at work; but the one who now holds it back will continue to do so till he is taken out of the way. And then the lawless one will be revealed, whom the Lord Jesus will overthrow with the breath of his mouth and destroy by the splendor of his coming. The coming of the lawless one will be in accordance with how Satan works. He will use all sorts of displays of power through signs and wonders that serve the lie, and all the ways that wickedness deceives those who are perishing. They perish because they refused to love the truth and so be saved. (2 Thessalonians 2:7–10)

Thus we learn how the beast's dominion shall be taken away and eventually be given to the saints of the Most High. But before the Lord Jesus Christ and His saints take dominion, the world will pass through a time of unbelievable suffering and oppression. The Scriptures point to the collapse of civilization as we know it before the second coming of Jesus Christ. As the old world order collapses, a new world order will arise. Humanity will invest its hopes in a single individual who arrives on the scene as a savior but who will ultimately be revealed as a fiend in human form.

As we look at the chaotic events of our own time, we have to wonder: How close are we to the events in this prophecy? Although it's impossible to say with precision, it's easy to believe that these events are just around the corner. Today, many world leaders are calling for a "new world order" with centralized power and global authority.

These calls for a one-world government are not new. Just five years after the end of World War II, British Prime Minister Winston Churchill delivered a speech in which he said, "The creation of an authoritative, all-powerful world order is the ultimate aim towards which we must strive. Unless some effective world super-Government can be set up and brought quickly into action, the prospects for peace and human progress are dark and doubtful."[1]

In our own time, we see a powerful movement toward a one-world government under a single leader. This movement is largely driven by the fear of nuclear war. Physicist Edward Teller, who led the US government's effort to develop the hydrogen bomb, later became an advocate for one-world government as a means of preventing nuclear war. In *The Legacy of Hiroshima*, he wrote, "Our goal in the final analysis cannot be merely to do away with arms and armies. We must, instead, work for the elimination of irresponsible and illegal acts of independent nations. We must work for the establishment of a world authority, maintained by moral force and physical force—a worldwide government capable of enforcing worldwide law and worldwide disarmament."[2]

In 1992, Strobe Talbott (who was later an official in the US State Department under President Clinton) predicted in *Time* magazine that within a century "nationhood as we know it will be obsolete; all states will recognize a single, global authority." The world would realize, he said, that "perhaps national sovereignty wasn't such a great idea after all."[3]

When anchorman Walter Cronkite accepted the 1999 Norman Cousins Global Governance Award at a United Nations ceremony, he said, "If we are to avoid the eventual catastrophic world conflict, we must strengthen the United Nations as a first step toward a world government. . . . To do that, of course, we Americans will have to yield up some of our sovereignty. That would be a bitter pill. It would take a lot of courage, a lot of faith in the new order." Cronkite added that a prominent "religious right" leader had declared that (in Cronkite's words) "we should have a world government but only when the Messiah arrives. Any attempt to achieve world order before that time must be the work of the Devil!"[4] Cronkite ridiculed this notion—but the books of Daniel and Revelation literally tell us that the "world order" that comes into existence before the Messiah returns truly *is* the work of the Devil.

Belgian-French civil servant Robert Muller served as assistant secretary general of the United Nations for four decades. He worked tirelessly to promote one-world government—and even a one-world *religion*—under the auspices of the UN. One of the ways he hoped to accomplish these goals was through a global ecological agenda. This statement from his website expresses the essence of his vision: "The United Nations must be vastly strengthened to resolve the major global problems . . . confronting humanity and the earth." He added that the UN "must be empowered to adopt and enforce world laws and regulations," and he urged world leaders to stand up and say, "The earth, our vital air, waters, nature, vegetation and many species . . . , our climate are in jeopardy. All this will end in a global disaster without precedent, if we do not react with vision and audacity."[5]

What sort of audacious and visionary action should the world take to prevent global disaster? "We must move as quickly as possible," Muller said, "to a one-world government; a one-world religion; under a one-world leader."[6]

Everywhere today there are increasing signs that we are facing an unprecedented world crisis—and soon. What's worse, it is not just one crisis we face, but a whole array of crises from which there is no escape no matter how hard we try. Yet all of these crises are completely of our own making. We are the ones who are polluting our own water, atmosphere, and environment. We are the ones who designed and built the atomic bomb and biological weapons and chemical weapons. It was the human race that devised terrorism and suicide bombing as a means to achieve religious and political ends. Famine is more often caused by government policies or wars than by crop failures and drought.

One of the most foolish and preventable crises we face today is the fiscal and economic crisis that now afflicts most Western nations, and especially the United States. We in the Western democracies elect representatives who are supposed to govern intelligently and responsibly. They presumably know how to add and subtract, and they know that if you spend more money than you take in, you are going to run up a lot of debt. Yet few of our elected representatives seem to worry about the national debt, and neither do the blissfully ignorant voters who vote for them. As a result, many Western democracies, from the United States to Spain and Greece, are accumulating levels of debt that can never be paid off. The debt is unsustainable—and when something is unsustainable, it must ultimately collapse.

Economists have been trying to warn us for years that Western civilization is on a *Titanic*-like course for disaster. Economist Michael Panzner warns that America is in rapid decline and nearing disaster. "The world's sole superpower," he says, is "afflicted with the overspending and overborrowing disease that has long been a distinguishing feature of ailing third world nations—and dying empires."[7]

Economist David M. Walker served as Comptroller General of the United States under Presidents Clinton and George W. Bush. In his book *Comeback America*, Walker warns that the sudden collapse of the Roman Empire should serve as a warning to all Americans:

> Many of us think that a super powerful, prosperous nation like America will be a permanent fixture dominating the world scene. We are too big to fail. But you don't have to delve far into the history books to see what has happened to other once-dominant powers. . . .
>
> Great powers rise and fall. . . . The millennium of the Roman Empire—which included five hundred years as a republic—came to an end in the fifth century after scores of years of gradual decay. . . .
>
> America presents unsettling parallels with the disintegration of Rome—a decline of moral values, a loss of political civility, an overextended military, an inability to control national borders, and the growth of fiscal irresponsibility by the central government. Do these sound familiar?[8]

British historian Niall Ferguson, author of *Civilization: The West and the Rest*, reminds us that when great empires such as Rome fell, the end came swiftly and without warning:

> What is most striking about this history is the speed of the Roman Empire's collapse. In just five decades, the population of Rome itself fell by three-quarters. Archaeological evidence from the late fifth century—inferior housing, more primitive pottery, fewer coins, smaller cattle—shows that the benign influence of Rome diminished rapidly in the rest of western Europe. . . . "The end of civilization" came within the span of a single generation.

> Other great empires have suffered comparably swift
> collapses. . . . [Empires] function in apparent equilibrium
> for some unknowable period. And then, quite abruptly,
> they collapse. . . . The shift . . . to destruction and then
> to desolation is not cyclical. It is sudden.[9]

The collapse of Western civilization will undoubtedly bring about conditions that send shock waves of fear around the globe. The frightened populace will welcome a strong leader who claims to care about people, who is an eloquent communicator, who leverages public opinion with the force of his personality, and who can accomplish apparent miracles with the invisible help of Satan himself. The economic crisis in Germany after World War I paved the way for the rise of Adolf Hitler. The much more frightening economic and social convulsions of our own future will pave the way for the rise of the Antichrist.

IDENTIFYING THE ANTICHRIST

Jeane Dixon (1904–1997) gained fame as an astrologer and self-proclaimed psychic from the 1950s through the 1990s. She claimed to be a devout Roman Catholic and said that her ability to foretell the future came from God. I believe her supposed "abilities" were actually the result of what has come to be called "the Jeane Dixon effect." The alleged "prophet" makes many predictions, some of which come true, and those that prove false tend to be forgotten.

For example, Jeane Dixon was interviewed for *Parade* magazine in 1956, and she predicted that the winner of the 1960 presidential election would be a Democrat and would "be assassinated or die in office," though, she added, "not necessarily in his first term."[10] On November 22, 1963, President John F. Kennedy was in fact assassinated during a motorcade through Dallas, Texas.

Yet people forget that Jeane Dixon had far more psychic misses than hits. In 1960, she actually contradicted her 1956 prediction, claiming that John F. Kennedy would lose the election. She also predicted that the Soviet Union would beat the United States to the moon and that the wife of Canadian Prime Minister Pierre Trudeau would give birth to a girl (despite 50/50 odds, she was wrong). If Jeane Dixon did have the ability to predict the future through astrology and psychic visions, the source of her knowledge would have to be demonic, not divine. But when you examine all the evidence, it becomes clear that her "predictions" were no more reliable than a coin flip.

So I have some misgivings as I share with you one prediction she made many years ago. I want to make it clear that I don't endorse Jeane Dixon or her predictions. On February 5, 1962, she claimed to have had a vision shortly before sunrise of a baby who would become a great leader. She explained:

A child, born somewhere in the Middle East shortly after 7 a.m. (EST) on February 5, 1962, will revolutionize the world. Before the close of the century he will bring together all mankind in one all-embracing faith. This will be the foundation of a new Christianity, with every sect and creed united through this man who will walk among the people to spread the wisdom of the Almighty Power.

This person, though born of humble peasant origin, is a descendant of Queen Nefertiti and her Pharaoh husband; of this I am sure. There was nothing kingly about his coming . . . no kings or shepherds to do homage to this newborn baby . . . but he is the answer to the prayers of a troubled world. Mankind will begin to feel the great force of this man in the early 1980s and during the subsequent ten years the world as we know it will be reshaped and revamped into one without wars or suffering. His power will grow greatly until 1999, at which time the people of this earth will probably discover the full meaning of the vision.[11]

Jeane Dixon claimed that this mysterious man would arise as the answer to millions of human prayers, and that he would become the founder of a new global religion, "a new Christianity" (suggesting that something is wrong with the old Christianity!). The fact that Jeane Dixon saw this individual—who would replace biblical Christianity with some "new Christianity"—makes it clear that her information is demonic in nature. Such a leader would probably seem to be a blessing at first, a strong and wise leader who guides the world out of chaos and into peace and security.

I know that as you read Jeane Dixon's words, you may feel a temptation to give credence and authority to them. You'll begin to wonder, "What if she is right? What if some great leader truly was born on February 5, 1962, and he is just awaiting his opportunity to step forth on the world stage?" Her description truly sounds like a description of the coming Antichrist—but only God knows the timetable of the great events that are coming upon the world in the last days. Satan may have given Jeane Dixon a few details that may prove correct—or her prediction may not contain a single scrap of truth. My point is that you should never trust a prophecy that doesn't come from God's Word.

Note, for example, that most of the dates Jeane Dixon gave in her prediction have already proven false. Jeane Dixon claimed that this man would leap onto the scene during the 1980s, and during the subsequent decade, he would radically impact the world, so that there would be no wars or suffering—and the whole world would discover the meaning of his vision by 1999. I certainly can't think of any person on the world scene today who fits that description. And we should always distrust any dates that are attached to any psychic vision. Psychics are no more authorized by God to set dates for the Antichrist than for the return of Jesus Christ.

But one thing is clear: The world is fast approaching a crisis, a time of unprecedented trouble in the world. We shall never again see anything that could be regarded as "normal times." So the question we have to ask ourselves as Christians is this: What kind of people should we be in times like these? This is exactly the question the apostle Peter asks in his second epistle: "Since everything will be destroyed in this way, what kind of people ought you to be? You ought to live holy and godly lives" (2 Peter 3:11).

On the first Palm Sunday, after Jesus was presented to Israel as the Messiah, He told the crowd in Jerusalem, "You are going to have the light just a little while longer. Walk while you have the light, before darkness overtakes you. Whoever walks in the dark does not know where they are going. Believe in the light while you have the light, so that you may become children of light" (John 12:35–36).

Though the world is growing dark, we have the light a while longer. We have the freedom to worship and study God's Word, and we can warm our souls in its light for a little longer. So let's believe in the light while we have the light. Let's live holy and godly lives so that we may become children of the light.

When the apostle Paul wrote to the Thessalonians believers, he encouraged them to be always ready for the Lord's return—to walk as children of the light. He wrote:

> Now, brothers and sisters, about times and dates we do not need to write to you, for you know very well that the day of the Lord will come like a thief in the night. While people are saying, "Peace and safety," destruction will come on them suddenly, as labor pains on a pregnant woman, and they will not escape.
>
> But you, brothers and sisters, are not in darkness so that this day should surprise you like a thief. You are all children of the light and children of the day. We do not belong to the night or to the darkness. So then, let us not be like others, who are asleep, but let us be awake and sober. For those who sleep, sleep at night, and those who get drunk, get drunk at night. But since we belong to the day, let us be sober, putting on faith and love as a breastplate, and the hope of salvation as a helmet. For God did

not appoint us to suffer wrath but to receive salvation through our Lord Jesus Christ. He died for us so that, whether we are awake or asleep, we may live together with him. Therefore encourage one another and build each other up, just as in fact you are doing. (1 Thessalonians 5:1–11)

We are not children of darkness but children of the light. Therefore we ought to live our lives in light of the fact that Jesus could return for us at any moment. Even though we live in turbulent times, we have nothing to fear if we are children of the light.

How would you live your life differently if you knew for certain that the Lord Jesus Christ was returning for you one month from today? How would it change your daily behavior? Would it change the way you spend your money? Would you purchase more luxuries, such as a new car or an expensive new boat? Or would you try a bit harder to reach friends and loved ones with the good news of Jesus Christ? Would you volunteer more time at the rescue mission, sharing your faith with people who have no hope? Would you visit people in the hospital and tell them that the Lord loves them and that He's coming soon?

Ask yourself how it would change your life to know for certain that the Lord is coming soon—*then make those changes in your life right now.* Start living today as if there were no tomorrow. Don't wait until "someday" to talk to your friends and loved ones about Jesus—*tell them right now.*

It's quite possible that the last Caesar, the Antichrist, is waiting in the wings right now, ready to step onto the stage of history. By studying the pages of the book of Daniel and the book of Revelation, as well as the other prophetic passages of the Bible, you make sure that you won't be fooled. Even while the rest of the world is caught up in deceit and delusion, you will know the truth and the truth will make you free.

The world is getting darker, but we are not depressed, discouraged, or downcast. Christians are not pessimists, because we know the end of the story: God wins. Satan loses. And we are on the winning side! So let us obey the Lord and lift up our hands and rejoice, because God is working out His eternal plan in human history.

And He is pleased to accomplish His plan through us.

6

THE GREAT PROPAGANDIST

Daniel 8

I n Daniel 2, the dream of Nebuchadnezzar provided a long-range telescopic view of history, beginning with Daniel's own era and continuing to a time that is still in our own future. In Daniel 7, the prophetic telescope zoomed in on events of the last days before our Lord's triumphant return. The prophetic symbols in Daniel's vision center on dramatic geopolitical events in the Mediterranean region in the last days. It should stir us and encourage us to realize that events still unfolding in our world today may be represented in the symbols in Daniel's vision.

Now we come to Daniel 8, and we encounter a vision of events that were in Daniel's future but have since been fulfilled in history. Within three centuries after the prophet Daniel experienced this vision, it was largely fulfilled. Yet the prophecy of Daniel 8 appears to have a double fulfillment. Although the vision we are about to explore has already been fulfilled, it awaits an even greater fulfillment yet to come.

There are many prophecies in Scripture that appear to have two prophetic meanings, a near-term fulfillment and a long-term fulfill-ment. For example, when Jesus, addressing His disciples, predicted the fall of Jerusalem (see Matthew 24:15–27), He was predicting events that occurred a mere forty years later, in AD 70, when the

Roman army under Titus Flavius conquered Jerusalem and demolished the temple.

Yet the historical fulfillment of the Lord's prophecy was a foretaste of a far more savage attack upon Jerusalem that is yet to come. In that future siege of Jerusalem, the nations will again surround and conquer the city. But in that future fulfillment of prophecy, Jerusalem will be delivered from its enemies by the return of Jesus Christ to the Mount of Olives. It is a double fulfillment—one fulfillment that has already occurred plus another more profound fulfillment yet to come.

This same principle of double fulfillment of prophecy is at work here in Daniel 8.

IN THE TIME OF WRATH

This chapter divides into two parts. First, we read the account of Daniel's vision of a ram and a goat in verses 1 through 14. As we see how history has accurately fulfilled this vision, our confidence in the reliability of God's Word is strengthened. Second, we read the interpretation of the vision, provided (as in Daniel 7) by the angel Gabriel. This future application of Daniel's vision may soon be fulfilled in our own time, right before our eyes.

Let's examine this vision together:

> In the third year of King Belshazzar's reign, I, Daniel, had a vision, after the one that had already appeared to me. In my vision I saw myself in the citadel of Susa in the province of Elam; in the vision I was beside the Ulai Canal. (Daniel 8:1–2)

Daniel begins by giving us the time and locale of the vision. Daniel experienced this vision two years after the previous vision in Daniel 7. This new vision came in the third year of King Belshazzar, while Babylon was still a powerful empire and before it was conquered by the Medes and Persians.

Daniel also described his location, though it is not clear whether he was physically present at this location or whether he pictured himself there in his vision. I am inclined to believe that the location he described was part of the vision, not his physical location, because he said that he was in Susa, the capital city of Persia, and that he stood by the Ulai Canal. I think it is extremely unlikely that Daniel was physically present in the capital city of the Persian Empire, which was an enemy of the Babylonian nation. The fact that he was standing beside the Ulai Canal may symbolize the fact that he was about to witness the flow of power from Persia toward the West, as predicted in Daniel's previous visions.

Daniel proceeds to relate what he saw in the vision:

> I looked up, and there before me was a ram with two horns, standing beside the canal, and the horns were long. One of the horns was longer than the other but grew up later. I watched the ram as it charged toward the west and the north and the south. No animal could stand against it, and none could rescue from its power. It did as it pleased and became great. (Daniel 8:3–4)

We do not need to wonder what this imagery means. It is interpreted for us later in this chapter by the angel Gabriel:

> While I, Daniel, was watching the vision and trying to understand it, there before me stood one who looked like a man. And I heard a man's voice from the Ulai calling, "Gabriel, tell this man the meaning of the vision."
>
> As he came near the place where I was standing, I was terrified and fell prostrate. "Son of man," he said to me, "understand that the vision concerns the time of the end."
>
> While he was speaking to me, I was in a deep sleep, with my face to the ground. Then he touched me and raised me to my feet.

> He said: "I am going to tell you what will happen later in the time of wrath, because the vision concerns the appointed time of the end. The two-horned ram that you saw represents the kings of Media and Persia." (Daniel 8:15–20)

The angel Gabriel's interpretation is clear and definite. He identifies the great ram as the Medo-Persian Empire, which would soon replace Babylon as the chief player on the stage of world power. Gabriel also uses phrases that suggest that Daniel's vision will have an additional fulfillment in the distant future: "understand that the vision concerns the time of the end," he says, and, "the vision concerns the appointed time of the end." That phrase "the time of the end" is consistently used in Scripture to refer to the time just before the return of Jesus Christ.

Gabriel also refers to "what will happen later in the time of wrath." The Hebrew word translated "wrath" is *za'am*, which means "anger" or "indignation." As used in Scripture, this word usually refers to God's indignation over the waywardness of His people Israel. It is a kind of measured anger you might feel toward someone you deeply love because that person has hurt you or disappointed you. There is a much stronger Hebrew word, *`ebrah*, which speaks of God's fury toward sin and rebellion. But here, Gabriel refers to God's indignation to designate a period of time that Jesus called the "great tribulation" (Revelation 7:14; cf. Matthew 24:21) and that the prophet Jeremiah called the time of Jacob's trouble (see Jeremiah 30:7). It will be a time when the nation of Israel experiences the indignation of God, just before the return of Jesus Christ.

ALEXANDER: THE KING WHO SAW HIMSELF IN PROPHECY

Daniel's vision continues:

> As I was thinking about this, suddenly a goat with a prominent horn between its eyes came from the west,

crossing the whole earth without touching the ground. It came toward the two-horned ram I had seen standing beside the canal and charged at it in great rage. I saw it attack the ram furiously, striking the ram and shattering its two horns. The ram was powerless to stand against it; the goat knocked it to the ground and trampled on it, and none could rescue the ram from its power. The goat became very great, but at the height of its power the large horn was broken off, and in its place four prominent horns grew up toward the four winds of heaven. (Daniel 8:5–8)

Again, the interpreting angel makes the symbolism of Daniel's dream clear. Gabriel explains:

"The shaggy goat is the king of Greece, and the large horn between its eyes is the first king. The four horns that replaced the one that was broken off represent four kingdoms that will emerge from his nation but will not have the same power." (Daniel 8:21–22)

History tells us that this is a description of the rise of the Greek empire under Alexander the Great (356–323 BC). Alexander, the brilliant son of Philip of Macedon, became the leader of his father's armies while he was still a teenager. After Philip was assassinated by the captain of his bodyguards, Alexander was proclaimed king at the age of twenty. He moved quickly to eliminate his rivals, consolidate his power, and expand his empire. He first led his armies north into the Balkans, then east into Asia Minor, which was then part of the Persian Empire. He continued his sweep into Syria and Palestine, then south into Gaza and Egypt, east into Assyria and Babylonian, across Persia and even into the Indian subcontinent.

Some nations, having suffered oppression under the Persians, viewed Alexander as a liberator. Others viewed him as a conqueror.

But wherever Alexander's armies went, the Persians were unable to stand before him, just as the vision of Daniel depicts. The "goat" that was Greece charged the "two-horned ram" of Persia, shattering its power, collapsing the empire, and trampling Persian lands underfoot.

There's an interesting historical footnote regarding Alexander the Great. The Roman-Jewish historian Josephus tells us that as Alexander rolled through Palestine on his march toward Egypt, he came against the city of Jerusalem. Josephus records that Alexander fully intended to conquer and plunder Jerusalem, and torture the high priest to death. But as Alexander approached the city, the priests of Jerusalem came out of the city to greet him.

The priests invited Alexander into the city and led him to the temple, where they opened a scroll of the book of Daniel to this very prophecy in Daniel 8. Josephus writes, "And when the Book of Daniel was showed him wherein Daniel declared that one of the Greeks should destroy the empire of the Persians, [Alexander] supposed that himself was the person intended. And as he was then glad, he dismissed the multitude for the present; but the next day he called them to him, and bid them ask what favors they pleased of him."[1]

Alexander also offered sacrifices to God in accordance with the high priest's directions. He treated the priests and populace of Jerusalem well, dispensing many favors, granting many requests. Alexander even enlisted many young men of Judea into his army, granting them the right to observe their own religious traditions and laws as they accompanied him in his wars of conquest.

Although this incident in history is not confirmed by any other historians, we do know that Jerusalem was one of the few cities in Alexander's path that he did not conquer but treated favorably instead. The use of Daniel's prophecy to win the favor of Alexander the Great is one of the most unusual uses of Bible prophecy in history.

Nearly a decade after sparing Jerusalem, Alexander was in the conquered city of Babylon, once the capital of the Babylonian empire. When he was in Babylon, Alexander would occupy the palace of Nebuchadnezzar II—the very palace were Daniel himself had served several Babylonian rulers. Alexander was in the palace for several weeks, planning new military campaigns (he was intent on an invasion of the Arabian Peninsula) while also drinking and reveling with his generals and advisors. The conqueror of the world could not conquer his own passions. In early June 323 BC, Alexander became deathly ill. Either someone poisoned his wine, or he contracted an illness such as typhoid or meningitis. He died at age thirty-two and left no heir.

As Daniel saw in his dream and Gabriel interpreted, the great horn of the shaggy goat, the king of Greece, was broken. The four horns that replaced the broken horn—Alexander's four top generals—represent four kingdoms that emerge from the broken kingdom that was Alexander's Greece.

All that was prophesied in Daniel 8 was later fulfilled in history.

JESUS AND THE SECOND FULFILLMENT

The description of Daniel's vision continues with still more historical events presented in symbolic form:

> Out of one of them came another horn, which started small but grew in power to the south and to the east and toward the Beautiful Land. It grew until it reached the host of the heavens, and it threw some of the starry host down to the earth and trampled on them. It set itself up to be as great as the commander of the army of the LORD; it took away the daily sacrifice from the LORD, and his sanctuary was thrown down. Because of rebellion, the LORD's people and the daily sacrifice were given over to it. It prospered in everything it did, and truth was thrown to the ground.
>
> Then I heard a holy one speaking, and another holy one said to him, "How long will it take for the vision to

be fulfilled—the vision concerning the daily sacrifice, the rebellion that causes desolation, the surrender of the sanctuary and the trampling underfoot of the LORD's people?"

He said to me, "It will take 2,300 evenings and mornings; then the sanctuary will be reconsecrated." (Daniel 8:9–14)

This prophecy has also been fulfilled. After the death of Alexander, a group of rivals known as the Diadochi ("Successors") battled each other for control of the vast kingdom Alexander had carved out. The Diadochi included some of Alexander's generals, family members, and friends. Among these were four generals, including one named Seleucus. He took as his portion the kingdom of Syria, which included much of Asia Minor (or Turkey, as it is known today). Another general, Ptolemy, took Egypt. These two generals were bitter enemies, and their two dynasties battled each other for many years. Because Syria was to the north of Palestine and Egypt to the south, Israel became a battlefield where these two implacable foes would meet and seek to destroy each other again and again.

The eighth king in the dynasty of the Seleucids, a descendant of Seleucus, was an incredibly evil man named Antiochus Epiphanes, who reigned from about 175 BC until his death in 164 BC. He has sometimes been called "The Antichrist of the Old Testament." Originally named Mithridates, he renamed himself Antiochus Epiphanes—"God Manifest"—after he gained the throne. This arrogant name gives you an insight into his personality.

His capital city in Syria was Antioch (named after Antiochus). You may recall that Antioch was the city in the New Testament where believers were first called Christians (see Acts 11:26). His behavior as king was so erratic and unpredictable that people began calling him "Antiochus Epimanes," Antiochus the Madman, a pun on the fact that the words *epiphanes* ("manifest") and *epimanes* ("madman") sound similar in Greek.

In the course of his many battles against Egypt, Antiochus Epiphanes conquered Jerusalem, removed the high priest, and installed his own corrupt priest. Later, when Antiochus was busy making war against Egypt, the deposed priest led an insurrection and forced the high priest appointed by Antiochus to flee. Enraged by the rebellion in Jerusalem, Antiochus attacked the city and ordered his soldiers to indiscriminately slaughter the people of Jerusalem—men and women, children and even infants. The historical record shows that forty thousand people were slaughtered outright and an additional forty thousand were sold into slavery.

Then, to punish the people who remained, Antiochus banned the Jewish religious observances, including the Sabbath, the feast days, and the sacrifices. A man could be put to death for simply saying, "I am a Jew." Mothers who had their baby boys circumcised were paraded through the city with their babes in arms, led to the top of the city wall, then mother and child were thrown off the wall to their deaths. Antiochus forced the Jews to sacrifice to Greek idols, and he tortured and executed anyone caught possessing the Hebrew Scriptures or keeping the Sabbath.

Antiochus also established "the rebellion that causes desolation" in the temple. He entered the temple and sacrificed an unclean animal—a pig—as an act of blasphemous worship of the Greek god Zeus. Then he took the fluids from the pig and sprinkled them around the sanctuary, defiling the temple. As a final act of desecration, he erected a statue of Zeus in the holy place.

These evil acts ended the twice-daily sacrifice, the continual burnt offering, in fulfillment of the prophecy of Daniel 8. In Daniel's prophecy, he saw "another horn, which started small but grew in power to the south and to the east and toward the Beautiful Land" (v. 9). This speaks of the growth of the power of Antiochus Epiphanes, who slaughtered the people of Jerusalem ("threw some of the starry host down to the earth and trampled on them," v. 10) and ended the continual burnt offerings ("took away the daily sacrifice from the LORD," v. 11). The interpreting angel told Daniel that the daily sacrifice would be suspended for "2,300 evenings and mornings; then the sanctuary will be reconsecrated" (v. 14).

This is a definite and precise prophecy. Many people reading this prophecy mistakenly think "2,300 evenings and mornings" means 2,300 days. But the prophecy does not say days because it does not mean days. The term "2,300 evenings and mornings" refers to 2,300 sacrifices. The continual burnt offering was made once each evening and once each morning, seven days a week. So 2,300 sacrifices, made twice each day, would equal 1,150 days, or just a little more than three years.

The book of 1 Maccabees (which contains a lot of historical information although it is not part of the Protestant canon of Scripture) records that the continual burnt offering ceased for a little more than three years. Finally, Judas Maccabaeus and his sons rose up and led the people in revolt. They retook the city of Jerusalem, cleansed the sanctuary, and restored the offerings at the end of 1,150 days, exactly as predicted in Daniel's vision. That is history.

But even though the prophecy of Daniel 8 has been fulfilled with regard to Antiochus Epiphanes, this prophecy still awaits a second fulfillment—a future fulfillment. As always, the second fulfillment is the larger and more globally significant fulfillment. The immense importance of the second fulfillment is suggested by some of the phrases used by the interpreting angel—and it is certified by the Lord Jesus himself. In Daniel 8:13, we read an unusual phrase, "the rebellion that causes desolation" (using the Hebrew word *pesha*, meaning "rebellion or transgression"). Later, in Daniel 9:27, the angel Gabriel will refer to this future fulfillment again, using a slightly different phrase, "an abomination that causes desolation" (instead of the Hebrew word *pesha*, meaning "transgression or rebellion," he uses *shiqquwts*, meaning "abomination or abominable idol").

And in Matthew 24:15, Jesus says, "So when you see standing in the holy place 'the abomination that causes desolation,' spoken of through the prophet Daniel . . . ," then you know that it is time to flee the city. Don't waste time, Jesus says, to go back for your coat—just run! Once the abomination that causes desolation is set up in the holy place, a time of great tribulation will come such as has never been seen since the world began. Jesus spoke those words more than one hundred sixty-five years after Antiochus Epiphanes had desecrated the temple, so He makes it clear that He is speaking of a second and future fulfillment of Daniel's prophecy.

A MASTER OF INTRIGUE

With these events in mind, let's take a closer look at what the angel Gabriel says about this future fulfillment:

> "In the latter part of their reign, when rebels have become completely wicked, a fierce-looking king, a master of intrigue, will arise. He will become very strong, but not by his own power. He will cause astounding devastation and will succeed in whatever he does. He will destroy those who are mighty, the holy people. He will cause deceit to prosper, and he will consider himself superior. When they feel secure, he will destroy many and take his stand against the Prince of princes. Yet he will be destroyed, but not by human power.
>
> "The vision of the evenings and mornings that has been given you is true, but seal up the vision, for it concerns the distant future." (Daniel 8:23–26)

This is a vivid and dramatic description. There are two factors in these words that mark the time of the fulfillment of the prophecy.

First, the angel says that it shall be in "the latter part of their reign" that this "fierce-looking king" shall arise. In the latter part of whose reign? Answers: The rulers who control the region once ruled by Antiochus Epiphanes—the region we know as Syria. This prophecy strongly suggests the reappearance of Syria at the crossroads of biblical and human history. Syria, one of the most advanced and important cultures in the Mediterranean region, was conquered by the Rashidun army in AD 640 and became part of the vast Umayyad Islamic Empire.

In 1516, Syria was conquered by the Ottoman Empire. After the Ottoman Empire was carved up by the European powers during World War I, Syria became a French mandate—and remained under French control until gaining full independence as a parliamentary republic in April 1946. So from AD 640 until 1946, the independent nation of Syria did not exist. Its history as a modern, independent state dates only from 1946.

Second, Gabriel says that there will be a time "when rebels have become completely wicked." I think the Revised Standard Version renders this phrase more accurately: "when the transgressors have reached their full measure." The English Standard Version also sheds more light: "when the transgressors have reached their limit." Evil can only go so far and no further, because God has set limits on how far evil people may go.

Gabriel here suggests that there will be a final crisis of history when transgression, corruption, violence, and lawlessness become so widespread and intense that God must call a halt. Evil has reached its full measure. At this point, when rebellion and transgression have reached their limit, a singular individual appears on the scene. According to Gabriel's description, he possesses two outstanding personal characteristics:

First, this individual is a "fierce-looking king." The Hebrew word translated "fierce-looking" is `az, which can indeed mean "fierce," but is more commonly translated "strong or mighty." So it might be more accurate to say that this individual projects a powerful personality. He has a commanding presence, a charismatic and magnetic appeal. He is a supremely confident leader, assertive and charming, and people are drawn to him.

Second, this individual is highly knowledgeable. He possesses the ability to understand riddles and to plan strategies that confound his opponents. He is, the New International Version says, "a master of intrigue." He is a natural psychologist, a master manipulator who understands what makes people tick. Using this knowledge and skill, he influences people in powerful ways.

Gabriel goes on to disclose this individual's method of operation. The angel says this man's power will be great, and he will succeed in everything he does—but not because of his own human power. He will exercise a derived power, a power that is not his own but that comes from another source. Gabriel does not specifically say that his power comes from a demonic source—but what other source could there be? And with that great power he will cause terrifying and widespread destruction.

This individual, the angel says, will cause devastation and destroy "those who are mighty, the holy people." He will target God's saints for destruction.

You will recall that in Daniel 7, we saw a beast that had ten horns—then an eleventh horn, a little one, appeared. This eleventh horn is a Caesar-like Roman-style political ruler who heads the Western confederacy of nations in the last days. We also saw that this eleventh horn is identified in Revelation 13 as the first beast. Here in Daniel 8, we see another vision of a little horn "which started small but grew in power . . . until it reached the host of the heavens, and it threw some of the starry host down to the earth and trampled on them . . . [and] took away the daily sacrifice from the LORD, and . . . prospered in everything it did, and truth was thrown to the ground" (Daniel 8:9–12). This little horn is also identified in Revelation 13, where John writes:

> Then I saw a second beast, coming out of the earth. It had two horns like a lamb, but it spoke like a dragon. It exercised all the authority of the first beast on its behalf, and made the earth and its inhabitants worship the first beast, whose fatal wound had been healed. (Revelation 13:11–12)

Here is *another* individual who exercises power in conjunction with the great political ruler of the last day. Note carefully what this individual is able to accomplish: "He will cause deceit to prosper, and he will consider himself superior. When they feel secure, he will destroy many and take his stand against the Prince of princes" (Daniel 8:25). He has an amazing ability to manipulate people and world events through the power of deception. Through his charm and charisma, he makes people *want* to believe his lies. He is a master of propaganda—the greatest propagandist in the history of humanity. He will undoubtedly be skilled in the use of mass communication techniques—television, radio, and the Internet—to broadcast his lies around the globe.

THE NEW ABOMINATION

Turning again to Revelation 13 we see that the great propagandist of Daniel 8 accords exactly with the second beast of John's vision:

> And it performed great signs, even causing fire to come down from heaven to the earth in full view of the people. Because of the signs it was given power to perform on behalf of the first beast, it deceived the inhabitants of the earth. It ordered them to set up an image in honor of the beast that was wounded by the sword and yet lived. The second beast was given power to give breath to the image of the first beast, so that the image could speak and cause all who refused to worship the image to be killed. It also forced all people, great and small, rich and poor, free and slave, to receive a mark on their right hands or on their foreheads, so that they could not buy or sell unless they had the mark, which is the name of the beast or the number of its name. (Revelation 13:13–17)

Here we see the most remarkable propaganda accomplishment in history. A great propagandist performs apparent miracles by which men and women are deceived and made to believe a lie.

The great propagandist convinces the people to erect an image in honor of the "first beast," who was wounded yet lived. This image is significant. Remember that Antiochus Epiphanes defiled the sanctuary of the temple in Jerusalem by erecting an image of Zeus. Put these passages together and it appears that we have a clear description of what occurs in the last days.

There has always been a question among Bible scholars as to which of the two beasts in Revelation 13 is actually the Antichrist. In my judgment, the first beast is the Antichrist. The second beast orders the image of the first beast to be set up—and then the second beast causes that image to come alive. It has the power of speech, and it also has the power to deal death to anyone who refuses to worship the image. Perhaps the animation of the image is accomplished by some future scientific advance—or perhaps it is accomplished by demonic power.

This image will be erected in the new temple to be built in Jerusalem. It will be the *new* abomination that makes desolation, as predicted by Jesus. It will mark the beginning of the terrible judgment of God.

By comparing Daniel 8 with Revelation 13, we can see more clearly how these two personages work closely together. One is a great and powerful political figure whose image appears in the temple to be worshiped as God. He does not personally appear in the temple, but his image is placed there by the agency of the second beast, who is the fulfillment of the little horn of Daniel 8.

The angel also says, "He will consider himself superior." In many ways, this individual will be a vastly magnified version of Antiochus Epiphanes, the arrogant dictator who renamed himself "God Manifest." He will be characterized by extreme narcissism—a preoccupation with his own power, prestige, and vanity, coupled with a wanton disregard for others and a willingness to destroy anyone who stands in his way. This narcissistic sense of superiority is reminiscent of the sin that led to the fall of Satan:

> How you have fallen from heaven,
>> morning star, son of the dawn!
> You have been cast down to the earth,
>> you who once laid low the nations!
> You said in your heart,
>> "I will ascend to the heavens;
> I will raise my throne
>> above the stars of God;
> I will sit enthroned on the mount of assembly,
>> on the utmost heights of Mount Zaphon.
> I will ascend above the tops of the clouds;
>> I will make myself like the Most High."
> But you are brought down to the realm of the dead,
>> to the depths of the pit. (Isaiah 14:12–15)

So it appears that this individual has fully given himself over to the spirit of self-adulation, self-obsession, and self-deification by which Satan fell. So the next line Gabriel speaks about this individual is hardly surprising: "When they feel secure, he will destroy many and take his stand against the Prince of princes" (Daniel 8:25). Who is the Prince of princes? It can only be Jesus himself, who is given the titles "King of kings and Lord of lords" and "ruler of the kings of the earth" in the New Testament (see 1 Timothy 6:15; Revelation 1:5; 17:14; 19:16).

The last sentence of Daniel 8:25 tells us the fate of this person: "Yet he will be destroyed, but not by human power." This second beast, the little horn of Daniel 8, faces the same doom as the first beast of Revelation 13. Their mutual fate is described in Revelation 19:

> Then I saw the beast and the kings of the earth and their
> armies gathered together to wage war against the rider on

the horse and his army. But the beast was captured, and with it the false prophet who had performed the signs on its behalf. With these signs he had deluded those who had received the mark of the beast and worshiped its image. The two of them were thrown alive into the fiery lake of burning sulfur. (Revelation 19:19–20)

The two "beasts" of Revelation, the Antichrist and the false prophet, are destroyed—but Gabriel says their destruction is "not by human power." Instead, they are "thrown alive into the fiery lake of burning sulfur." Daniel and John, writing six hundred years apart, both agree that these two powerful figures will deceive and amaze the whole world at the time of the end—then they will be destroyed.

ABOUT THE KING'S BUSINESS

Having witnessed this vision, and having heard the interpretation of the vision by the angel Gabriel, Daniel describes a profound effect this vision has had upon his body, soul, and spirit:

I, Daniel, was worn out. I lay exhausted for several days. Then I got up and went about the king's business. I was appalled by the vision; it was beyond understanding. (Daniel 8:27)

The prophet Daniel was sickened by all that he had seen. He was so physically exhausted that he was unable to function for several days. Despite the toll this vision took on him, he didn't let it deter him from his duties. He arose and did his job. He went about the king's business.

When I read Daniel's concluding words in chapter 8, I'm reminded of the words of the Lord Jesus to His disciples when He told them a parable about His second coming: "Occupy till I come"

(Luke 19:13 KJV). In other words, the Lord told His disciples that they should go about the King's business until the King returns.

Once, after I had spoken in church about Bible prophecy and the last days, someone said to me, "If I knew for sure that these were the last days, I think I would live a lot differently than I do." Can you identify with those words?

The Lord wants us to know that it should make no difference whatsoever if we are certain or not that we live in the last days. The Lord could return for us at any moment. Every generation that has lived since the Lord's first appearance on earth could easily have been the last. That's why every generation has expected Christ's return.

Since the Word of God continually reminds us of our responsibility to go about the King's business at all times, every Christian who has ever lived during these past two thousand years will be judged as to whether he or she has taken God's Word seriously. Whether or not we are approaching the times prophesied by Daniel and the book of Revelation, the forces that will usher in the time of the Antichrist have been at work in every generation. We should live every day as if God himself has told us that we are in the last days. We should be about the King's business every day.

Are you completely available to God? Have you surrendered all your rights and privileges to the lordship of Jesus Christ? Have you presented your body as a living sacrifice to Him? As the apostle Paul reminds us, Jesus "died for all, that they which live should not henceforth live unto themselves, but unto him which died for them, and rose again" (2 Corinthians 5:15 KJV).

We have been bought with a price; we are no longer our own. Therefore, the only reasonable thing we can do is present ourselves for Him to use as He pleases. That is the choice that truly gives life meaning. In light of eternity—in light of all the Lord has done for us—let us be about the King's business. Let us occupy till He returns.

—7—

GOD'S COUNTDOWN

Daniel 9

On April 25, 1961, NASA prepared to launch an Atlas rocket with a space capsule on its nose. Inside the space capsule was a robotic, mechanical astronaut in a space suit. The mission was intended to gather information that would be used to launch human astronauts in the future. Mission Control counted down to zero, and the Atlas rocket lifted off the launchpad. Forty seconds into its flight, the rocket veered off course and had to be destroyed, although the space capsule was recovered from the ocean.

Three days later, on April 28, NASA prepared another rocket for launch. It too had a space capsule on the nose, but no astronaut. Mission Control counted down to zero and the rocket lifted off. Thirty-three seconds into its flight, the rocket went off course and had to be destroyed. The space capsule was again retrieved.

Just one week later, on May 5, NASA again prepared to launch a rocket—a Redstone rocket with a Mercury space capsule on the nose. This time, however, the space capsule, christened *Freedom 7*, had a human being inside—Commander Alan Shepard. Once again, Mission Control began its countdown.

As the countdown proceeded toward zero, Commander Shepard tried not to think about the two failed rocket launches of the preceding days. Finally, the countdown reached zero. The engines fired. The rocket lifted off the launchpad, and it carried the first American astronaut into space. The suborbital flight lasted fifteen minutes, and it carried Shepard to an altitude of one hundred sixteen miles. *Freedom 7* splashed down in the Atlantic about three hundred miles from the launch site. Shepard came home to a hero's welcome.

Countdowns are nerve-racking, even for astronauts with the "right stuff." And countdowns are nerve-racking for you and me as we count down the final stages of human history. God has a countdown, and it is ticking steadily toward the most crucial moment since the creation of the world.

But the countdown to the return of Jesus Christ is not the only timetable God has had for human history. In Daniel 9, we encounter one of the few places in Scripture where God ties himself to a definite timetable of events. This passage of Scripture is one of the strongest proofs of the reliability and divine inspiration of God's Word.

THE MESSIANIC TIMETABLE

Has anyone ever asked you, "Why do you believe the Bible is the Word of God?" Every Christian should live in such a way that, from time to time, people ask you what you believe and why you believe it. It's helpful to know certain passages of Scripture that clearly set forth a prophetic prediction and a historic fulfillment. The reason such passages are important is that a prediction fulfilled centuries later can only be made by divine foreknowledge and fulfilled by divine power.

Here in Daniel 9 we see one of the most dramatic examples of such passages. These prophetic verses pinpoint the exact moment in history when the Jewish Messiah would present himself to the Jewish people. This prophecy was written more than five hundred years before the event took place. The Daniel 9 prophecy is so clear and detailed that it has always been an acute embarrassment to those who would criticize the Scriptures and deny the accuracy of Bible prophecy.

Leopold Hoffman Cohn came from an Orthodox Jewish community in Berezna, Hungary. In 1880, at age eighteen, he graduated from a talmudic academy, planning to become a rabbi. One of his daily rituals was to repeat the Thirteen Articles of Maimonides. The twelfth article is a profession of faith in the coming of the Messiah.

As Cohn continued studying the Hebrew Scriptures and reading the rabbinical commentary known as the Talmud, he wrestled with questions and doubts regarding the Messiah. According to his studies, the Messiah should have come to Israel long ago. And as he read in Daniel 9, it struck him like a thunderbolt that Daniel had predicted that the arrival of the Messiah would take place less than five centuries after the prophecy was given—yet the rabbis all agreed that Messiah had not come.

Cohn went to an older rabbi, one of his mentors, and asked him how to resolve the contradiction. The rabbi told him that it was a question that should not be asked—and that if he continued pursuing such questions, he could destroy his career as a rabbi. But Leopold Cohn could not let the matter go.

In 1892, Cohn left Hungary and immigrated to the United States, settling in New York City. One day, he was walking by a church and he noticed a sign that read, "Meetings for Jews." He went inside and a Jewish Christian gave him a copy of the New Testament.

Leopold Cohn took the New Testament home and read it straight through in a single marathon session from morning until past midnight. By putting the New Testament together with his deep understanding of the Old Testament, especially the book of Daniel, Cohn concluded that Jesus—or *Yeshua*, His Hebrew name—was in fact the Messiah the Jewish people had waited for. He fell to his knees and received Jesus as his Lord and Savior.

Cohn became an ordained minister and founded the Brownsville Mission to the Jews (now called Chosen People Ministries).

He became one of the early leaders in the Messianic Judaism movement—and it all began because a young Jewish scholar dared to ask forbidden questions about Daniel 9.

The prophecy in Daniel 9 is not a vision or a dream. It was not given to Daniel through any means that we have already witnessed in this book. It was spoken directly to Daniel by the angel Gabriel. It's appropriate that Gabriel is the same angel who appeared to Joseph and to Mary, announcing the birth of Christ. Here in Daniel 9, Gabriel is sent to Daniel to give him a clear glimpse of the future, including God's timetable for the arrival of the Messiah.

DANIEL'S PRAYER

It's significant that Gabriel is sent in answer to Daniel's prayer. The first part of the chapter, Daniel 9:4–19, is taken up with that prayer. It is a masterpiece of worship, adoration, confession, petition, and intercession.

Daniel received this prophecy, he tells us, after Babylon fell to the Medes and Persians. He writes:

> In the first year of Darius son of Xerxes (a Mede by descent), who was made ruler over the Babylonian kingdom—in the first year of his reign, I, Daniel, understood from the Scriptures, according to the word of the LORD given to Jeremiah the prophet, that the desolation of Jerusalem would last seventy years. So I turned to the Lord God and pleaded with him in prayer and petition, in fasting, and in sackcloth and ashes. (Daniel 9:1–3)

By this time, Daniel was an old man, almost ninety years of age. He had been reading in the book of the prophet Jeremiah. These words provide a valuable insight, because they show us that Daniel studied the Scriptures. Though he was a prophet and God spoke directly to him, he was nevertheless a student of the Scriptures.

Where God has spoken in writing, he does not add a vision. So, through his study of Jeremiah, Daniel realized that Israel's Babylonian captivity was nearly at an end. Here is the passage Daniel read:

> This is what the LORD says: "When seventy years are completed for Babylon, I will come to you and fulfill my good promise to bring you back to this place." (Jeremiah 29:10)

Jeremiah had prophesied that the Jewish people would be captives in Babylon for seventy years. Daniel had been a teenager when the Babylonians conquered Jerusalem and took him in chains to Babylon. He had lived through the full seventy years that God had ordained for Israel's captivity. So Daniel realized that the time of Israel's deliverance was near, and he began to pray on the basis of the promise of God.

Daniel's prayer tells us a great deal about how we should pray. Prayer is not merely going to God and asking Him for what we want—though God does hear us when we petition Him in prayer. The primary purpose of prayer is not to align God with our will but to align our will with His. Through prayer, we volunteer to serve God's agenda. How do we discover God's program? By studying God's Word.

When Daniel learned what God's program was for the Jewish people, he prayed that God might give him a role to play in this wonderful thing He was about to do. He prayed a prayer of adoration toward God and a prayer of confession, identifying himself with the sins of his people. He asked God to show mercy and forgiveness toward Israel, so the Jewish people could go home and restore their desolate city, Jerusalem.

Daniel did not take an attitude that said, "Well, this prophecy in Jeremiah is going to happen. It's right there in black and white. There's no point in praying about it." Daniel knew that God's promise was sure and that Jeremiah's prophecy would be fulfilled—but Daniel prayed because he did not want to be left out. He wanted to play a part in God's plan to change the world. Prayer is the most important way in which we become involved in God's agenda. Here is the prayer Daniel prayed:

> I prayed to the LORD my God and confessed:
>
> "Lord, the great and awesome God, who keeps his covenant of love with those who love him and keep his commandments, we have sinned and done wrong. We have been wicked and have rebelled; we have turned away from your commands and laws. We have not listened to your servants the prophets, who spoke in your name to our kings, our princes and our ancestors, and to all the people of the land.
>
> "Lord, you are righteous, but this day we are covered with shame—the people of Judah and the inhabitants of Jerusalem and all Israel, both near and far, in all the countries where you have scattered us because of our unfaithfulness to you. We and our kings, our princes and our ancestors are covered with shame, LORD, because we have sinned against you. The Lord our God is merciful and forgiving, even though we have rebelled against him; we have not obeyed the LORD our God or kept the laws he gave us through his servants the prophets. All Israel has transgressed your law and turned away, refusing to obey you.
>
> "Therefore the curses and sworn judgments written in the Law of Moses, the servant of God, have been poured out on us, because we have sinned against you. You have fulfilled the words spoken against us and against our rulers by bringing on us great disaster. Under the whole heaven nothing has ever been done like what has been done to Jerusalem. Just as it is written in the Law of Moses, all this disaster has come on us, yet we have not sought the favor of the LORD our God by turning from

our sins and giving attention to your truth. The LORD did not hesitate to bring the disaster on us, for the LORD our God is righteous in everything he does; yet we have not obeyed him.

"Now, Lord our God, who brought your people out of Egypt with a mighty hand and who made for yourself a name that endures to this day, we have sinned, we have done wrong. Lord, in keeping with all your righteous acts, turn away your anger and your wrath from Jerusalem, your city, your holy hill. Our sins and the iniquities of our ancestors have made Jerusalem and your people an object of scorn to all those around us.

"Now, our God, hear the prayers and petitions of your servant. For your sake, Lord, look with favor on your desolate sanctuary. Give ear, our God, and hear; open your eyes and see the desolation of the city that bears your Name. We do not make requests of you because we are righteous, but because of your great mercy. Lord, listen! Lord, forgive! Lord, hear and act! For your sake, my God, do not delay, because your city and your people bear your Name." (Daniel 9:4–19)

Daniel's prayer is a model for all of us who are concerned about the decline and decay of our nation. We look around us and we see immorality, corruption, deception, and spiritual corrosion. Our leaders do not acknowledge God, and they are leading our nation off a cliff. So what do we do? We complain. We rant and rave. We feel like kicking the TV set. But do we pray?

If you truly care about your country, then I would encourage you to read through this prayer and apply it to your own world, your own nation, your own state, and to yourself as a citizen. Encourage fellow believers to pray this prayer. How might our nation be changed if Christians everywhere would pray the prayer of Daniel?

"THE ROSETTA STONE OF BIBLICAL PROPHECY"

Daniel was interrupted as he prayed, and he didn't finish all that he intended to pray. He described that interruption in the next few verses:

> While I was speaking and praying, confessing my sin and the sin of my people Israel and making my request to the LORD my God for his holy hill—while I was still in prayer, Gabriel, the man I had seen in the earlier vision, came to me in swift flight about the time of the evening sacrifice. He instructed me and said to me, "Daniel, I have now come to give you insight and understanding. As soon as you began to pray, a word went out, which I have come to tell you, for you are highly esteemed. Therefore, consider the word and understand the vision." (Daniel 9:20–23)

Notice especially Gabriel's exhortation to "consider the word and understand the vision." This is highly significant in view of the reference Jesus himself makes in His prophetic message on the Mount of Olives shortly before His crucifixion. There He refers to this prophecy of Daniel and says, "So when you see standing in the holy place 'the abomination that causes desolation,' spoken of through the prophet Daniel—" (to which Matthew adds his own parenthesis, "let the reader understand" (Matthew 24:15). In this way, Jesus indicated how His followers (whether in the first century, the twenty-first century, or the hundred-and-first century) might know that the time of the end had arrived. This is a clear exhortation on the part of both Gabriel and the Lord Jesus, and readers should take care to consider and understand this passage.

Someone has properly called Daniel 9 "the Rosetta Stone of biblical prophecy." Everything else in Scripture must fit into the outline of this great prophetic revelation. All other Bible prophecy is validated by this prophetic passage.

This prophecy, found in verses 24 through 27, divides into two parts. The first part lists the objectives that will be accomplished during the course of the prophecy. The second part sets forth a three-fold division of this climactic time in human history. Let's examine the first section of this prophecy:

> "Seventy 'sevens' are decreed for your people and your holy city to finish transgression, to put an end to sin, to atone for wickedness, to bring in everlasting righteousness, to seal up vision and prophecy and to anoint the Most Holy Place." (Daniel 9:24)

The first section of this prophecy presents three profound insights.

First, the angel Gabriel tells Daniel (and us) that a specific period of time has been decreed. "Seventy 'sevens' are decreed for your people and your holy city," he says. The Hebrew word that is translated *sevens* is *shabuwa`*, which literally means "weeks." A week of days is seven days, so a week of years would be seven years. Seventy weeks of years, then, would be seventy times seven, or a total of four hundred ninety years that have been decreed or apportioned for Daniel's people. Clearly, this refers to the nation of Israel.

Second, when the angel speaks of "your holy city," he is clearly speaking of Jerusalem. So this prophecy is clearly limited to a period of time when the people of Israel possess and occupy the holy city of Jerusalem. This timetable has no effect if the Jews do not occupy Jerusalem. So, for example, this timetable could not have been fulfilled at any time between AD 70 and AD 1967, because throughout all of those years, the Jews did not occupy Jerusalem.

Third, the angel Gabriel identifies six specific goals God will accomplish during this period of four hundred ninety years. These goals divide into two parts.

The first three goals deal with the work of redemption: "to finish transgression, to put an end to sin, to atone for wickedness." All three of these goals have to do with the solution to the problem of sin. These three goals were accomplished through Jesus Christ.

The next three goals deal with the final realization of the hopes and dreams of the human race: "to bring in everlasting righteousness, to seal up vision and prophecy, and to anoint the Most Holy Place."

The goal of bringing in everlasting righteousness refers to establishing the kingdom of God—the kingdom we pray for in the Lord's Prayer: "Your kingdom come, your will be done, on earth as it is in heaven" (Matthew 6:10). That is what it means to bring in everlasting righteousness.

The next goal is "to seal up vision and prophecy." The Hebrew phrase translated "to seal up" means to complete something and bring it to an end. This means that all predictions are to be completed and fulfilled in the course of this period of four hundred ninety years, and there will be no longer any need to predict a future event.

The final goal is "to anoint the Most Holy Place." This is a reference to the temple in Jerusalem. There must be a temple in Jerusalem in order for these four hundred ninety years to be fulfilled. If the temple in Jerusalem did not exist at the end of that time, the prophecy could not be fulfilled.

This gives us an overall view of the prophecy. The full course of the prophecy would take place over a period of four hundred ninety years. At the end of that time, the problem of human sin would be solved. A full and complete atonement for wickedness would be made.

THE MOST PRECISE PREDICTION EVER MADE

The second section of this prophecy sets forth a threefold division of the four hundred ninety years. The first two divisions are described in verse 25:

> "Know and understand this: From the time the word goes
> out to restore and rebuild Jerusalem until the Anointed

One, the ruler, comes, there will be seven 'sevens,' and sixty-two 'sevens.' It will be rebuilt with streets and a trench, but in times of trouble." (Daniel 9:25)

Here Gabriel says that there will be a definite starting point when the four hundred ninety years begin. It will be a clearly identifiable historical event. That event is identified as the time when a decree goes forth to restore and rebuild the city of Jerusalem.

The books of Ezra and Nehemiah record several decrees by Persian kings concerning Israel, but two of them clearly relate to the building of the temple. The temple was built before the city walls were restored. There is only one decree (recorded in Nehemiah 2) that gave permission to the Jews to rebuild the walls and the city of Jerusalem, and that decree is dated with precision.

Here we encounter one of those remarkable "coincidences" that are really not coincidences at all, for we learn that the Greek historian Herodotus (known as "the Father of History") was a contemporary of the Persian king Artaxerxes, who issued the decree. Both Herodotus and another great historian of that era, Thucydides, record the career and dates of Artaxerxes. So the actions of this king are clearly recorded for us in historical records outside of the Scriptures. When secular history intersects with biblical history, even the critics of the Bible must acknowledge the validity of God's Word.

According to Nehemiah 2, the decree to rebuild Jerusalem was issued in the twentieth year of the reign of Artaxerxes. We can pinpoint that precisely as occurring in the year 445 BC.

Some Bible commentators have made the mistake of selecting a different starting point. They date the year of the decree, the twentieth year of Artaxerxes, as 454 BC. This is because they follow the timeline of Archbishop James Ussher, the seventeenth-century Irish bishop who calculated a chronology of biblical history and took it upon himself to insert dates into our Bible (for example, he determined that the creation of the world took place on Sunday, October 23, 4004 BC). Archbishop Ussher has been proven wrong with regard to many of his dates, and this is especially true of his date 454 BC for Artaxerxes' twentieth year. Secular historians have never accepted that date, but all agreed that Artaxerxes' twentieth year was 445 BC. This is the correct starting point of the four hundred ninety years. Those who use 454 BC as the starting point find the termination for the first sixty-nine weeks takes place at AD 29 or 30, which some people regard as the year of the first Palm Sunday, when Jesus was presented to Israel as King.

The angel Gabriel also indicates that this four hundred ninety-year period will contain two divisions. The first division consists of seven "weeks" of seven years, or forty-nine years. During that forty-nine year period, the city is rebuilt "with streets and a trench [or moat], but in times of trouble." History has fulfilled this prophecy. Jerusalem was rebuilt, the walls were repaired, and the city was restored.

After the first division of forty-nine years comes the second division of sixty-two "weeks" of years, or four hundred thirty-four years. Add these years to the forty-nine years, and they total four hundred eighty-three years "until the Anointed One, the ruler, comes." In the Hebrew Bible, the word *Mashiah* or *Mashiach* literally means "anointed one," and it refers to a liberator or savior who comes as a king or priest who has been anointed with holy oil.

This is by far the most precise and finely tuned prediction ever made in the Bible or in any other sacred literature of any religion. The angel Gabriel tells Daniel that precisely four hundred eighty-three years after the decree to rebuild Jerusalem is issued, the Messiah will appear to the nation of Israel. The countdown began 445 BC, and it continued counting down for exactly four hundred eighty-three years *to the exact month*.

How do we know the exact month? We know because the decree to rebuild Jerusalem was issued in the Hebrew month Nisan, which corresponds to April. You can read about the Persian king's decree in Nehemiah 2, which begins, "In the month of Nisan in the twentieth year of King Artaxerxes . . ." To find the fulfillment of the prophetic timetable that Gabriel gave to Daniel, you move to the first Palm Sunday in April AD 32. In counting the years, you must use the ancient three hundred sixty day year (the standard calendar year of the ancient Egyptians, Babylonians, and Hebrews), not the three hundred sixty-five day year we observe today.

If you work out this chronology with care, you find that exactly four hundred eighty-three years after the decree to rebuild Jerusalem, the Lord Jesus entered the city of Jerusalem, riding on a donkey. As He came into the city, a huge crowd greeted Him, spreading their cloaks and palm branches on the road before Him. And the people shouted, "Hosanna to the Son of David!" and "Blessed is the king of Israel!" (see Matthew 21:9; Mark 11:8–10; Luke 19:37–38; and John 12:13.)

When Jesus entered Jerusalem in this way, He fulfilled the timetable of Daniel 9:25, and He also fulfilled the prophecy of Zechariah:

> Rejoice greatly, Daughter Zion!
> Shout, Daughter Jerusalem!
> See, your king comes to you,
> righteous and victorious,
> lowly and riding on a donkey,
> on a colt, the foal of a donkey. (Zechariah 9:9)

That first Palm Sunday is often referred to as the "triumphal entry" of Jesus into Jerusalem. Yet Luke's gospel tells us that as Jesus approached Jerusalem and saw the city, He wept over it and said, "If you, even you, had only known on this day what would bring you peace—but now it is hidden from your eyes" (Luke 19:42).

What kind of a triumphal entry is this? Jesus wept over the city! And notice that Jesus says, "If you . . . had only known *on this day* what would bring you peace." Why did Jesus specifically say "on this day"? It's because that very day was the fulfillment of the four hundred eighty-three years of God's prophetic timetable. That was the day God's countdown reached zero.

Jesus went on to say, "The days will come upon you when your enemies will build an embankment against you and encircle you and hem you in on every side. They will dash you to the ground, you and the children within your walls. They will not leave one stone on another, because you did not recognize the time of God's coming to you" (Luke 19:43–44).

Here the Lord predicts the destruction of the city—and His prophecy was fulfilled four decades later by the Roman general Titus. All of this happened, Jesus said, "because you did not recognize the time of God's coming to you."

The people of Jerusalem should have known. Gabriel had disclosed, and Daniel had faithfully recorded, the exact time when Messiah would come—but the people did not recognize the time when God came to them as their king. They prided themselves on being students of Scripture yet, as Jesus said to them, "You study the Scriptures diligently because you think that in them you have eternal life. These are the very Scriptures that testify about me" (John 5:39).

On Sunday the people shouted, "Blessed is the king of Israel!" On Friday, the mob shouted, "Crucify Him! We have no king but Caesar."

A STRANGE INTERLUDE

Earlier, we noted that the period of four hundred ninety years is divided into three parts. We just examined the first two of those divisions. The first division consisted of the forty-nine years of the rebuilding of the city of Jerusalem. The second division consisted of the sixty-two "weeks" of years, or four hundred thirty-four years, from the rebuilding of Jerusalem to the triumphant arrival of the Anointed One, Jesus the Messiah, in Jerusalem.

This leaves a final seven-year period before the completion of the four hundred ninety years. That seven-year period is the third division. But before the seven-year period begins, there is a strange interlude, an indeterminate period of time. The angel Gabriel speaks of that interlude in the next verse:

> "After the sixty-two 'sevens,' the Anointed One will be put to death and will have nothing. The people of the ruler who will come will destroy the city and the sanctuary. The end will come like a flood: War will continue until the end, and desolations have been decreed." (Daniel 9:26)

The Anointed One, Jesus the Messiah, entered the city of Jerusalem right on schedule at the conclusion of the "sixty-two 'sevens,'" the four hundred eighty-three years. Then, Gabriel says, "the Anointed One will be put to death and will have nothing." Just days after the Lord's triumphal entry into the city, everything He had was taken from Him. He literally had nothing, and He was nailed to a cross. Then He was lifted up against the sky on a little hill outside the Damascus gate on the north side of the city.

He came to offer himself as King to a nation that had been told for centuries of His coming. Instead of a crown, they gave Him a wreath of thorns. Instead of a kingly scepter, they shoved a broken reed into His hands. Instead of a throne, they gave Him a bloody cross to die on. He was the Creator and Sustainer of the universe. He left everything, and He had nothing.

On that cross He fulfilled the prophecy Gabriel gave to Daniel that during the time of the "seventy 'sevens,'" God would finish transgression, bring an end to sin, and make an atonement for wickedness. All of this was fulfilled when the Anointed One was put to death on the cross outside the city of Jerusalem.

And Gabriel went on to tell Daniel, "The people of the ruler who will come will destroy the city and the sanctuary. The end will come like a flood: War will continue until the end, and desolations have been decreed."

The "ruler who will come" is another prophecy with a double fulfillment. In one sense, it is a reference to the fourth kingdom of Nebuchadnezzar's dream in Daniel 2, a kingdom that would be "strong as iron—for iron breaks and smashes everything." It's also a reference to the "fourth beast" of Daniel 7, a "terrifying and frightening and very powerful" beast with "large iron teeth," a beast that "crushed and devoured its victims and trampled underfoot whatever was left." These are references to the Roman Empire. And in AD 70, forty years after the Lord's crucifixion, the Roman general Titus led the iron-fisted Roman army against Jerusalem. The Romans broke the walls of Jerusalem, entered the city like a flood, smashed everything, crushed the people, destroyed the temple, and trampled underfoot whatever remained.

It was one of the most horrifying events in all of human history, and it was recorded for us by Josephus—the Jerusalem-born Jewish historian who defected to the Romans in AD 67, when he was captured in Galilee during the First Jewish-Roman War. He served as a translator to Titus during the Siege of Jerusalem in AD 70. After failing to convince the Jewish rebels to surrender to the Romans, he was an eyewitness to the siege, slaughter, and destruction of Jerusalem and its temple.

Josephus describes the terrible weeks of siege before the Roman army actually entered the city. The Romans had completely surrounded Jerusalem so that there was no commerce, no one going in or out, and no food supply. Famine stalked the streets of the city. People died by the hundreds, and there was no place to bury them, so the corpses were stacked up in the streets. Mothers ate the flesh of their own children to survive.

Finally, the city was overthrown. The Roman soldiers, infuriated by the stubborn resistance of the Jews, pillaged and burned the temple. The fire was so intense that many of the gold and silver implements of worship melted, and the molten metal ran down into the cracks between the stones. Later, the soldiers pried the stones apart to retrieve the gold and silver—and thus they fulfilled the Lord's prophecy that not one stone of the temple would be left standing upon another (see Matthew 24:2; Mark 13:2; Luke 19:44; 21:6).

This was the first fulfillment of the double prophecy in Daniel 9:26. The second fulfillment is yet to come and will take place at the end of the seventieth week of this prophecy.

But what happened to that seventieth week? Why didn't it take place immediately after the sixty-ninth week? If that final period of seven years had followed the sixty-ninth week without a break, the entire four hundred ninety years of the prophecy would have ended seven years into the events of the book of Acts. But there is no account in Acts of an event that suggests an end to the four hundred ninety years.

Clearly, there is a gap, an indeterminate period of time, between the sixty-ninth week and the seventieth week. During this gap of time, the Romans destroyed the city of Jerusalem, the church was founded and grew, the gospel was preached and spread around the world, centuries passed—and the countdown toward that final week, the seventieth week of years, has steadily continued. In fact, it still continues. We don't know when that countdown will reach zero. The angel Gabriel gave Daniel a timetable for the first arrival of Jesus the Messiah—but only God the Father knows a timetable for His return.

Before the Messiah returns in triumph, the Antichrist will rise and lead the world toward destruction. As we saw in Daniel 7, the Antichrist will be the last Caesar of the Roman world. And here we see the second fulfillment of the doubly fulfilled prophecy: "The people of the ruler who will come will destroy the city and the sanctuary." The armies of the Roman world—the Western world—will come to destroy Jerusalem again.

But when will that happen? So far, nearly two thousand years have come and gone since the end of the sixty-ninth week of years— a vast gap of time between the first four hundred eighty-three years of the Daniel 9 prophecy and the final seven years. We are living in that gap, and God's countdown continues.

Some Bible scholars reject the notion of a gap between the sixty-ninth and seventieth weeks. After all, Daniel does not mention any gap, does he? Actually, he does—but you must read the text with extreme care in order to see it.

The concluding event, the climax, of the first sixty-nine weeks was the Lord's triumphal entry into Jerusalem. That event brought the sixty-nine weeks (the "seven 'sevens,' and sixty-two 'sevens.'") to a close. Then, Daniel 9:26 tells us, *"After the sixty-two 'sevens,' the Anointed One will be put to death."* Daniel does not say that the Messiah is executed near the end of the sixty-nine weeks but *after* the sixty-nine weeks. In the original Hebrew, the term translated "after" uses a conjunction combined with a preposition, which would better be translated "then after." Such wording creates a chronological full stop, a pause, a gap, after the sixty-nine weeks. The Messiah was actually crucified in the opening days of this indeterminate gap in time. So, even though the reference is subtle, Daniel does mention a gap of time after the close of the sixty-nine weeks.

The idea of an indeterminate gap of time between the sixty-ninth and seventieth weeks of this prophecy is not a recent invention. At the beginning of the third century, the renowned Christian theologian Hippolytus of Rome, commenting on this very prophecy of Daniel, wrote, "By one week, therefore, he [Daniel] meant the last week which is to be at the end of the whole world."[1] So the interpretation of an indeterminate interlude between the sixty-ninth and seventieth weeks was part of mainstream Christian theology at least as far back as the third century AD.

THE END OF THE COUNTDOWN

Next, the angel Gabriel relates to Daniel what will take place when God's countdown reaches zero, and the final week of Daniel's prophecy is fulfilled:

> "He will confirm a covenant with many for one 'seven.'
> In the middle of the 'seven' he will put an end to sacrifice
> and offering. And at the temple he will set up an abomi-
> nation that causes desolation, until the end that is decreed
> is poured out on him." (Daniel 9:27)

Who is "he"? Who is this strange individual Gabriel refers to? "He will confirm a covenant with many for one 'seven.'" This must be someone who has already been mentioned in the prophecy, or the angel would not have used a pronoun to identify him. Grammatically, the nearest antecedent to the pronoun is the reference in the preceding verse to "the ruler who will come."

This ruler will confirm a covenant, a binding agreement with "many." Who are the "many"? As I write these words, the answer is not clear. In the future, when this prophecy is fulfilled, I think it will be abundantly clear who the "many" are. Some speculate that the "many" might refer to the nations that make up the confederacy of Western nations descended from the old Roman Empire.

Others speculate that the "many" might refer to all the nations of the earth. For example, a global economic collapse might cause the entire world to turn to this ruler for salvation. This ruler, the Antichrist, might confirm a covenant with the "many" to create a "cashless currency" that is recognized throughout the world. According to this covenant, the global "cashless currency" could take the form of a mark on the right hand or forehead of all citizens, as John described in his apocalyptic vision:

> Because of the signs it [the second beast] was given power to perform on behalf of the first beast, it deceived the inhabitants of the earth. . . . It also forced all people, great and small, rich and poor, free and slave, to receive a mark on their right hands or on their foreheads, so that they could not buy or sell unless they had the mark, which is the name of the beast or the number of its name. (Revelation 13:14, 16–17)

Is John's reference to "the inhabitants of the earth . . . all people, great and small" a parallel to the angel's reference, related by Daniel, to the ruler who will "confirm a covenant with many for one 'seven'"? I don't know. This is certainly a reasonable theory.

However, I lean toward the view that the "many" refers to the nation of Israel, the Jewish population. In any case, the term of the covenant that the Antichrist makes is for seven years. In the midst of that seven-year period—after only three and a half years—this ruler "will put an end to sacrifice and offering." At that point, this ruler will set up "an abomination that causes desolation" in a restored temple in Jerusalem. This is what the Lord Jesus spoke of when He said:

> "So when you see standing in the holy place 'the abomination that causes desolation,' spoken of through the prophet Daniel—let the reader understand—then let those who are in Judea flee to the mountains. Let no one on the housetop go down to take anything out of the house. Let no one in the field go back to get their cloak. How dreadful it will be in those days for pregnant women and nursing mothers! Pray that your flight will not take place in winter or on the Sabbath. For then there will be great distress, unequaled from the beginning of the world until now—and never to be equaled again." (Matthew 24:15–21)

Here the Lord Jesus gives us His commentary on Daniel 9:26–27. It's clear that we can expect to see the rise of a confederacy of Western nations, culturally descended from the fourth kingdom, the Roman Empire. This confederacy may be taking shape today. It will ultimately come to be dominated by this strange individual who has appeared in these prophetic passages. He will make an agreement with the Jews as a nation, and it is possible that this agreement will result in the construction of a new temple on the Temple Mount. That is why the entire Christian world continually watches Israel and hangs on every rumor concerning the reconstruction of the temple on the ancient site. The temple must be rebuilt before these final events can occur.

The statement, "He will confirm a covenant with many" seems to refer to an agreement to permit the restoration of Jewish worship in Jerusalem. At the exact midpoint of the seven-year period, "he will put an end to sacrifice and offering." Why? Because, in his infinite arrogance, he will demand that the worship due to God be given to himself. So this last of the Roman Caesars will set up an image of himself in the temple, and he will demand to be worshiped as God. This is what both Jesus and the angel Gabriel call "the abomination that causes desolation." And the desolation in Jerusalem will continue "until the end that is decreed is poured out" in judgment upon the Antichrist.

We know what the end of the Antichrist will be. John describes the judgment and fate of the Antichrist in Revelation 19:20, where he writes that the Antichrist will be "thrown alive into the fiery lake of burning sulfur." And Paul writes that the end of the Antichrist will take place at the return of Jesus Christ: "And then the lawless one will be revealed, whom the Lord Jesus will overthrow with the breath of his mouth and destroy by the splendor of his coming" (2 Thessalonians 2:8).

The prophet Zechariah tells us that the Lord's return will occur at the exact same spot where He left the earth following His resurrection: "On that day his feet will stand on the Mount of Olives, east of Jerusalem, and the Mount of Olives will be split in two from east to west, forming a great valley, with half of the mountain moving north and half moving south" (Zechariah 14:4). At the moment of His arrival, the Lord will begin to wreak vengeance upon the nations assembled against Jerusalem—especially against this blasphemous individual who has gained control of the world.

There is no room for doubting the validity of these prophecies, because they have been partially fulfilled in precise accuracy concerning the first appearance of the Lord Jesus Christ. If the arrival of the Messiah was predicted and fulfilled with such startling pinpoint accuracy, then we can be assured that the entire prophecy will be fulfilled in the end. God's countdown is proceeding, and when it reaches zero, everything will happen exactly as predicted, with clockwork precision.

A CONTINGENT PLAN

How do we explain the reason for that strange interlude of history, the long gap between the sixty-ninth and seventieth weeks of Daniel's prophecy? Why does God permit this long parenthesis of time to interrupt the four hundred ninety years of His prophetic timetable?

I believe that the only explanation is that there is an element of contingency in God's timetable. When God says something will happen, it will happen. The fulfillment is sure—but the exact timing of its fulfillment is contingent upon the behavior of human beings and their reaction to the prophecy. We see a similar principle at work in other passages of Scripture.

For example, in the book of Jonah, the prophet Jonah went to Nineveh and prophesied against the city. "Forty more days," he declared, "and Nineveh will be overthrown" (Jonah 3:4). But the people of Nineveh responded to Jonah's message and they repented. From the king down to the humblest citizen, the Ninevites put on sackcloth and ashes, and they repented before God of their wickedness. As a result, forty days passed and nothing happened. God suspended and delayed the fulfillment of His prophecy, spoken through Jonah.

In much the same way, I believe there is an element of contingency in Daniel's prophecy. One of the great mysteries of our faith is the fact that God is absolutely sovereign over human history, yet He also gives human beings free will. In some paradoxical fashion beyond our understanding, God's sovereign predestination interacts with human free will in a way that always accomplishes God's purposes.

We catch a glimpse of this principle at work in the book of Acts, where Peter preaches to the people after the healing of a lame man at the temple gate. Peter says:

"Now, fellow Israelites, I know that you acted in ignorance, as did your leaders. But this is how God fulfilled what he had foretold through all the prophets, saying that his Messiah would suffer. Repent, then, and turn to God, so that your sins may be wiped out, that times of refreshing may come from the Lord, and that he may send the Messiah, who has been appointed for you—even Jesus. Heaven must receive him until the time comes for God to restore everything, as he promised long ago through his holy prophets." (Acts 3:17–21)

This is why the gospel was to be preached to the Jews first and then to the Gentiles, as recorded in the letters of Paul. The good news of Jesus Christ had to go to the Jews first, after the day of Pentecost, so that they might be given an opportunity to receive their Savior. Had they done so, it is highly possible that this entire prophetic scheme of the seventy weeks of years (four hundred ninety years) would have been fulfilled in that day, and the earth would have long since moved into and beyond a time of millennial peace. But God created us with free will, He respects human free will, and He weaves human decisions into His program for history. His plan for human history can never be thwarted—but He does permit certain events to be contingent on human actions and decisions.

Will God's plan for human history be fulfilled in our day? We cannot know for sure. Just when it seems that historic events are about to usher in the end times, many people may make a choice to obey God and serve Him, and like the Ninevites, their obedient choices may move God to suspend His countdown for a time and move back His timetable for judgment.

Ultimately, the last days will come. The end of history will be marked, as Jesus indicated, by a stubborn refusal of people to take God's warnings seriously. As Jesus said to His disciples, "When the Son of Man comes, will he find faith on the earth?" (Luke 18:8). Will He find anyone who still believes in God and conducts his life accordingly? Who knows what those days will bring? God alone knows.

God's timetable reminds me of NASA's timetable each time the space agency prepared to launch a rocket into space. Sometimes the countdown proceeded smoothly to zero. But more often, the scientists would detect a problem with weather conditions or with the rocket itself. So they would have to put the countdown on hold. Once the problem was resolved, the countdown could continue.

God has been counting down ever since the twentieth year of Artaxerxes. For a time of four hundred eighty-three years, the countdown ran its course. The Savior appeared right on schedule. It seemed as if the end of history was a mere seven years away. But then something happened. The countdown was delayed. It will resume once more when the temple again stands on the Temple Mount in Jerusalem. At some point, the last Roman Caesar will erect a blasphemous image in the temple, "the abomination that causes desolation." When that happens, the end will be near.

What does this mean to you and me?

It means it's time to take seriously the days in which we live. It makes no difference if we are already in the last days, or if Jesus will not return for a thousand or ten thousand years. We are responsible to obey the Word of God and to serve His program, no matter how long it will be until it is fulfilled. We don't need to know God's timetable. We don't need to know the exact moment when the countdown reaches zero.

Our only job is to be ready when that moment arrives.

8

THE OTHER SIDE OF PRAYER
Daniel 10

Dr. Helen Roseveare was an English missionary to the Congo from 1953 to 1973. In 1964, during the civil war in the Congo, rebels took her prisoner and repeatedly beat and raped her. She later recalled that she survived the horrors of that ordeal through prayer. She talked to God—and she sensed His answer within her.

One night, the rebels savagely kicked and beat her in her own home. She recalled, "The Lord seemed to whisper to me: 'They are not beating you, but Me-in-you. These are not your sufferings, but Mine.'" She said she sensed "the consciousness of His loving arms around me and His peace in my heart, even in the midst of wickedness and suffering—the sense of being privileged to share in the fellowship of His sufferings."

After five months of captivity, Dr. Roseveare was rescued by soldiers. When you hear Dr. Roseveare's story, you wonder how anyone could endure such a brutal and terrifying ordeal, and still be able to trust in God. She believes her faith was strengthened by an amazing incident during her first few years as a missionary in Africa.

An African mother had died in childbirth, leaving Dr. Roseveare to care for a premature baby. The baby was dying because Dr. Roseveare didn't have a means of keeping the baby warm. Had the baby been born in Europe or the United States, she would have been placed in a nice, warm infant incubator. But in Africa in the 1950s, doctors had to improvise. Normally, a simple hot water bottle would have done the trick, but the last bottle on hand had burst when the nurse tried to fill it.

So Dr. Roseveare placed the baby in a box and surrounded her with cotton wool, then placed the box near the fireplace. She told the nurses to keep the fire hot and protect the baby from cold drafts.

The next day, Dr. Roseveare went to visit an orphanage, as she did most days. She told the children about the tiny baby and how they needed a hot water bottle to keep the baby warm. Then she prayed with the children. One orphan girl, ten-year-old Ruth, prayed, "Please, God, send us a water bottle today. Tomorrow will be too late, so please send it this afternoon. And while You are about it, please send a dolly for the little girl so she'll know You really love her. Amen."

Helen Roseveare couldn't bring herself to believe that God would answer such an audacious prayer. The hospital rarely received packages—and who would ever think to send a hot water bottle to a country on the equator?

Later that afternoon, Dr. Roseveare was teaching at the nurses' training school when a package arrived. Somehow, she knew that Ruth's prayer had been answered. She sent for the orphanage children to come help her open the package. Together, they pulled off the twine, opened the cardboard flaps, and lifted out donated clothing, bandages, and packages of food. Feeling down near the bottom of the box, she pulled out a brand-new rubber hot water bottle. Little Ruth shouted, "If God has sent the bottle, He must have sent the dolly too!" Dr. Roseveare reached to the bottom of the box—and found a beautiful dolly for the baby. Ruth asked, "Can I give this dolly to the baby so she'll know that Jesus really loves her?"

The box had been shipped five months earlier from Dr. Roseveare's home church in England. God had used those Christians to answer a child's prayer that would be prayed *five months after the box was packed.* The baby lived—and Dr. Helen Roseveare never doubted the power of prayer again—not even during the brutal five-month ordeal of her captivity.[1]

In the tenth chapter of the book of Daniel, we turn from prophecy to prayer. Many people feel a bit let down at this point. Prophecy is exciting—but we find it hard to get excited about studying prayer. But if we truly understand the revolutionary power of prayer, we will realize that this chapter contains one of the most exciting and life-changing insights we will ever encounter.

DOWN TO THE RIVER TO PRAY

We should be careful not to be confused by chapter divisions in the final three chapters of Daniel. These three chapters, Daniel 10 through 12, make up one grand vision of the future.

As Daniel 10 opens, the prophet Daniel calls a prayer meeting. He begins by preparing himself and devoting himself for a time of intense, heartfelt, urgent prayer to God. What prompts him to undertake this intense devotion to prayer? He is in trouble. Daniel writes:

> In the third year of Cyrus king of Persia, a revelation was given to Daniel (who was called Belteshazzar). Its message was true and it concerned a great war. The understanding of the message came to him in a vision.
>
> At that time I, Daniel, mourned for three weeks. I ate no choice food; no meat or wine touched my lips; and I used no lotions at all until the three weeks were over.
>
> On the twenty-fourth day of the first month, as I was standing on the bank of the great river, the Tigris, . . . (Daniel 10:1–4)

Later, in verse 7, Daniel mentions "those who were with me." In other words, Daniel had gathered a number of people together on the banks of the Tigris River for a prayer meeting. Since ancient times, rivers have been powerful spiritual metaphors that speak to the believer's heart. When Daniel and his fellow believers gathered on the banks of the Tigris, they were much like the believers in the old spiritual that calls all people, brothers and sisters, fathers and mothers, children and sinners, "down to the river to pray."

As Daniel prepared himself for the prayer meeting, it was as if he were observing Lent. He had given up all delicacies, all meat and wine and desserts, for a period of three weeks. In fact, he had probably not even bathed in that time, because anointing oneself with lotions or scented oils was part of the bathing process in that day.

Why did Daniel devote himself to fasting? He did so because he was troubled. He didn't go without eating and bathing in order to impress God with how spiritual he was. God is not impressed by our attempts to make ourselves seem righteous by our own actions. And he didn't fast in order to impress other people about how spiritual he was. As Jesus said in the Sermon on the Mount:

> "When you fast, do not look somber as the hypocrites do, for they disfigure their faces to show others they are fasting. Truly I tell you, they have received their reward in full. But when you fast, put oil on your head and wash your face, so that it will not be obvious to others that you are fasting, but only to your Father, who is unseen; and your Father, who sees what is done in secret, will reward you." (Matthew 6:16–18)

Daniel was no hypocrite. He was not trying to impress anyone. His fasting was an act of mourning over sin and humbling himself before the Lord. He was removing distractions so he could focus his mind and heart entirely on God. The Scriptures give us many good and righteous reasons for fasting in addition to praying. In Daniel 9:3, we saw that Daniel prayed, fasted, and pleaded with God when he learned from the book of Jeremiah that the desolation of Jerusalem was almost at an end, and he wanted God to use him in the divine plan to rebuild Jerusalem.

The Scriptures also contain examples of fasting when we are mourning a loss (2 Samuel 1:12), seeking God's guidance (Ezra 8:21), repenting from sins (Jonah 3:5), preparing for spiritual warfare (Matthew 4:1–2), or listening intently for the voice of God (Acts 13:2–3). Here in Daniel 10, the prophet Daniel was undoubtedly seeking God's guidance, preparing for spiritual battle, and listening for God's voice as he went without food, wine, and certain basics of life in order to devote himself fully to God for a period of time.

TOPAZ AND BLINDING LIGHT

In verse 1, Daniel tells us why he was troubled: It was the third year of the reign of Cyrus, King of Persia—and that was a significant date. The time had come that was predicted by the prophet Jeremiah—the end of the seventy years of Israel's captivity and Jerusalem's desolation. Although the seventy years were ended, Daniel saw no sign that the people of Israel were allowed to leave Babylon—or even wanted to.

In Palestine, the Hebrews had been an agricultural people, keeping herds of cattle and flocks of sheep. But when they were taken captive to Babylon, they could no longer practice their former trade. They learned the commercial trades of Babylon. Once a nation of sheepkeepers, they had become a nation of shopkeepers. They were making so much money running the Babylonian equivalent of Macy's and JC Penney that many had no intention of returning to Palestine.

But Daniel knew that it was God's program for his people to return and rebuild their temple, their city, and their nation. They could never be blessed and fulfilled as a people while neglecting God's promise that they would return to Palestine.

Out of his great concern for his nation, Daniel gathered some faithful friends together at the river, and he called a prayer meeting. He wanted God to stir up His people to return to Palestine. Daniel and his friends probably arrived at the riverbank with long faces and heavy hearts. But as they prayed together, an amazing thing happened. Daniel describes what happened next:

> On the twenty-fourth day of the first month, as I was standing on the bank of the great river, the Tigris, I looked up and there before me was a man dressed in linen, with a belt of fine gold from Uphaz around his waist. His body was like topaz, his face like lightning, his eyes like flaming torches, his arms and legs like the gleam of burnished bronze, and his voice like the sound of a multitude. (Daniel 10:4–6)

As they prayed, Daniel suddenly saw an amazing figure of a man standing before him dressed in linen. He describes this figure in startling terms. He appears to be made out of the precious gemstone topaz, a transparent crystal that comes in a variety of colors, from yellow to orange to pink and blue. The man's face shines with a blinding light. His voice sounds like many voices speaking at once. Who can this man be?

We are reminded of the One described by John the apostle in the book of Revelation. In the opening chapter of his vision, John saw this amazing figure:

> I turned around to see the voice that was speaking to me. And when I turned I saw seven golden lampstands, and among the lampstands was someone like a son of man, dressed in a robe reaching down to his feet and with a golden sash around his chest. The hair on his head was white like wool, as white as snow, and his eyes were like blazing fire. His feet were like bronze glowing in a furnace, and his voice was like the sound of rushing waters. In his right hand he held seven stars, and coming out of his

mouth was a sharp, double-edged sword. His face was like the sun shining in all its brilliance. (Revelation 1:12–16)

Daniel saw his vision while standing by the Tigris River in Babylon. John saw his vision centuries later while exiled on the island of Patmos. Although these men were separated by time and geography, their visions were remarkably similar. Both men were praying as these visions occurred—and as they prayed, a curtain opened. That curtain was the barrier that separates us from the invisible spiritual kingdom. When the curtain fell away, they could see the very One they had been speaking to in prayer.

That Person didn't suddenly appear out of nowhere—He had been there all the time, but He had been invisible. Through prayer, the veil that cloaked Him from Daniel's eyes was pierced. Daniel's eyes were opened. He saw the invisible world of spiritual beings around him—and he suddenly beheld the One whose eyes were like flaming torches and whose face shone like the sun in its strength.

Daniel could not have fully understood who this man clothed in linen was—but in the book of Revelation, John clearly identifies this Person, not by name but by description:

When I saw him, I fell at his feet as though dead. Then he placed his right hand on me and said: "Do not be afraid. I am the First and the Last. I am the Living One; I was dead, and now look, I am alive for ever and ever! And I hold the keys of death and Hades." (Revelation 1:17–18)

In all of human history, only one Person has ever earned the right to be called "the First and the Last," the One who was dead, and is now "alive for ever and ever," and who possesses "the keys of death and Hades." That one Person is the Lord Jesus Christ, and He has revealed himself to both Daniel and John in a marvelous way, unveiling the glory and majesty of His being.

THE ONE WHO IS IN US

One of the strangest aspects of Daniel's vision by the river concerns the people who were with him:

> I, Daniel, was the only one who saw the vision; those who were with me did not see it, but such terror overwhelmed them that they fled and hid themselves. So I was left alone, gazing at this great vision; I had no strength left, my face turned deathly pale and I was helpless. Then I heard him speaking, and as I listened to him, I fell into a deep sleep, my face to the ground. (Daniel 10:7–9)

Although Daniel could see this amazing Person who seemed to be made of topaz, burnished bronze, and lightning, his companions could not. Even so, his companions sensed that awe-inspiring supernatural power had been unleashed in their midst. Maybe they heard the Lord's voice. Or maybe the power of His presence struck a responsive chord deep in their souls. In any case, though they could not see what Daniel saw, they were seized with terror, and they fled the scene.

This isn't the first time something like this has happened. There is a similar story in 2 Kings 6. There the prophet Elisha and his servant were in the little town of Dothan in Palestine. The king of Aram was at war with the nation of Israel. But every time Aram prepared to attack, Elisha would send word to the king of Israel and warn him to be on guard. So Aram was thwarted and defeated again and again.

Infuriated, the king of Aram sent forth his army to capture Elisha. The army came by night, as Elisha slept, and surrounded the town of Dothan with soldiers, horses, and chariots. When Elisha's servant awoke the next morning, he looked out and saw the army that surrounded the city, and he panicked.

But Elisha calmly replied, "Don't be afraid. Those who are with us are more than those who are with them" (v. 16). Then the prophet prayed, asking God to open the servant's eyes—and instantly the servant saw that the hills were filled with horses and chariots of fire. Then Elisha asked God to strike the army of Aram with blindness, and it was done.

This is what the New Testament means when it says, "the one who is in you is greater than the one who is in the world" (1 John 4:4). The One who is in us is invisible to the world, hidden behind the curtain that hides the spiritual realm from human eyes. But sometimes God pulls the curtain aside, and the invisible becomes astoundingly, even terrifyingly, visible. Daniel experienced such a moment when he saw with his own eyes the One to whom he had been praying.

Saul of Tarsus, before he became the apostle Paul, had a similar experience on the road to Damascus. At the time, he was a violent persecutor of the Christian church. In fact, he was on his way to Damascus in Syria to take charge of some Christians in that city. He planned to bring them back to Jerusalem to stand trial for the "crime" of believing in Jesus Christ. But there on the road a sudden light shone brighter than the noonday sun. At that moment, Saul saw the Lord Jesus.

How did Saul react to what he saw? Like Daniel, he fell to the ground. Like Daniel's companions, Saul's companions could not see the Person of Jesus—but they did hear the voice that spoke to Saul. Scoffers and skeptics have tried to explain away the experience of Saul on the Damascus road, claiming he simply had an epileptic seizure. When this "explanation" was reported to the English evangelist Charles Haddon Spurgeon, he replied, "O blessed epilepsy! Would that every man in London could have epilepsy like that!"

So it was with Daniel. Overwhelmed by the majesty of the One who stood before him, Daniel realized the limitless power he had tapped into through the ministry of prayer. The voice of this Person had a profound effect on Daniel: "Then I heard him speaking, and as I listened to him, I fell into a deep sleep, my face to the ground" (Daniel 10:9).

Daniel is not saying that this Person's words droned on and put him to sleep. No, he's saying that His words were so powerful, His voice was so mesmerizing, that Daniel fell into a spiritual trance as a prelude to a profound revelation. God was preparing the prophet Daniel to learn a remarkable and profound insight. Daniel had already witnessed the majesty of Jesus Christ. Now he would learn the mystery of prayer.

THE ANGEL ARRIVES

After Daniel witnesses this manifestation of the preincarnate Lord Jesus Christ, another important figure arrives on the scene—an angel of the Lord. This angel gives us a profound glimpse into the mysterious workings of prayer. Daniel explains:

> A hand touched me and set me trembling on my hands and knees. He said, "Daniel, you who are highly esteemed, consider carefully the words I am about to speak to you, and stand up, for I have now been sent to you." And when he said this to me, I stood up trembling.
>
> Then he continued, "Do not be afraid, Daniel. Since the first day that you set your mind to gain understanding and to humble yourself before your God, your words were heard, and I have come in response to them. But the prince of the Persian kingdom resisted me twenty-one days. Then Michael, one of the chief princes, came to help me, because I was detained there with the king of Persia. Now I have come to explain to you what will happen to your people in the future, for the vision concerns a time yet to come." (Daniel 10:10–14)

Some people confuse this being with the first person Daniel saw, the man clothed in linen with a face that shone like the lightning. This being is an angel, sent by the man clothed in linen to help Daniel. The angel touches Daniel and helps him to his feet. Daniel rises, trembling and shaking, and the angel reveals to him a number of profound insights about prayer. These insights have been given to us so that we might learn what takes place behind the scenes when we pray.

The New Testament tells us that angels are "ministering spirits sent to serve those who will inherit salvation" (Hebrews 1:14). God sends them to meet the needs of believers. Think of all the times when you were spared from catastrophe by some seeming "quirk of fate" or "coincidence." Most Christians have had dozens, even hundreds of such close calls. If the truth were known and the curtain were pulled back to reveal the invisible workings of the spiritual world, you would discover that you were not spared by a "coincidence"—you were spared by an angel. God's angels are constantly ministering to us, whether we are aware of them are not.

Here in Daniel 10, the prophet Daniel has his eyes opened to the vast invisible world that lies behind prayer. This angel has come to reveal startling truths about the invisible world of the spiritual realm.

The first revelation: The moment Daniel began to pray, God began to answer. The angel said, "Do not be afraid, Daniel. Since the first day that you set your mind to gain understanding and to humble yourself before your God, your words were heard, and I have come in response to them" (v. 12). God sent Daniel's answer immediately. This is the first insight the angel teaches about prayer. The moment we pray, the answer is on its way.

Of course, this doesn't mean God will always answer in the way we want or expect. Daniel prayed to God on the basis of the will of God. The purpose of prayer is not to bend God to our will, but to submit our will to His. Prayer is the means by which we become involved in God's agenda.

That's why the prayer Jesus taught us in the Sermon on the Mount is so simple. He didn't teach us that prayer is a shopping list. Prayer is volunteering for duty. It's like saying, "Lord, give me an assignment, a mission to perform, a job to do in Your Kingdom." Jesus taught us to pray:

"Our Father in heaven,
hallowed be your name,
your kingdom come,
your will be done,
   on earth as it is in heaven.
Give us today our daily bread.
And forgive us our debts,
   as we also have forgiven our debtors.
And lead us not into temptation,
   but deliver us from the evil one."

(Matthew 6:9–13)

That prayer asks very little of God—daily bread, forgiveness, and deliverance from evil. Everything else in that prayer is praise, praying for the Kingdom, praying for the fulfillment of God's will, and a commitment to a lifestyle of forgiveness. Nowhere in that prayer does Jesus suggest that we need to beg or harangue God in prayer. Nowhere does the Lord suggest that we need to set up a picket line around God to force Him to give in to us. Prayer is not a protest demonstration. We do not need to twist God's arm and besiege Him with a flood of words until He gives in.

Jesus warns against praying in vain repetitions, "babbling like pagans" who "think they will be heard because of their many words" (see Matthew 6:7). Just as God knew in advance that a newborn baby would need a hot water bottle and a dolly, He knows what we need before we ask Him. So when we go to God in prayer, we are not there to inform God as to what He ought to do. We do not pray to advise God, enlighten God, or bring Him up to speed on what He needs to do. He knows already. In fact, one of the most important things we need to do in prayer is to *listen*, so that we can become involved in accomplishing His agenda.

God wants us to ask Him to do what He says He will do—and He often will not do it at all unless we ask Him. That's why James says, "You do not have because you do not ask God" (James 4:2). If you would ask Him, God would do what He promises to do. He is eager to fulfill His promises to you, but He wants to have a relationship with you. He wants to be asked.

GOD'S ANSWER—DELAYED

The angel told Daniel, "Since the first day that you set your mind to gain understanding and to humble yourself before your God, your words were heard, and I have come in response to them" (10:12). In other words, when we pray on the basis of God's will, His answers are immediate and sure. This reminds us of something Jesus taught us about prayer. He said, "Ask and it will be given to you; seek and you will find; knock and the door will be opened to you" (Matthew 7:7).

Ask. Seek. Knock. These are three forms of prayer. Sometimes when we pray, we simply need to ask. At other times, we need to seek, we need to investigate and study, we need to understand what God is doing. And there are also times when we must knock, which involves repetition—not the "vain repetition" and babbling of ritualized and formulated prayer, but earnestly and repeatedly laying our hearts open before the Lord.

Different circumstances demand different forms of prayer. We need only ask for wisdom, love, power, and grace, and God will give them to us (see James 1:5). And Jesus promised that everyone who earnestly seeks will find, and everyone who knocks will see the door opened (see Matthew 7:8). The answers are sure when we pray on the basis of what God has said He will do. That is what the angel made clear to Daniel.

But the angel went on to explain to Daniel that delays sometimes occur. In the case of Daniel's prayer, God sent His answer immediately, but the answer did not arrive for three weeks. What held it back? The angel says, "But the prince of the Persian kingdom resisted me twenty-one days" (10:13).

Who is this "prince" in Persia? This is a reference to a fallen angel. There are good angels who serve God and help God's people—but there are also evil, rebellious angels, also called demons, and they continually oppose what God is doing. Many of these demons are invisible rulers of the affairs of certain nations of the earth. This passage, which reveals these truths, helps us to understand much of what is reported in the daily news.

Why are some nations seemingly bent on doing evil and stirring up trouble in the world? Why are some nations full of hate toward God's chosen people and the nation of Israel? Why do some nations practice violence, oppression, murder, and genocide as a matter of state policy? It's not merely that the *human* leaders of those nations have given themselves over to sin and evil. More importantly, the *demonic* rulers of those nations are invisibly at work, controlling the minds and hearts of men.

That's why evil things happen in the world. As Paul reminds us, "For our struggle is not against flesh and blood, but against the rulers, against the authorities, against the powers of this dark world and against the spiritual forces of evil in the heavenly realms" (Ephesians 6:12). We tend to think that we are at war with evil people. Capitalists blame the leftists and the leftists blame the capitalists. Republicans blame the Democrats and vice versa. Labor and management blame each other. Husbands and wives blame each other. Parents and children blame each other. Faculty and students blame each other, and the administration blames both.

Paul reminds us that in spiritual warfare people are not the enemy. Our enemies are invisible. They are the rulers, authorities, powers, and spiritual forces of the invisible spiritual realm. That is what the angel tells Daniel. Behind all the visible problems, tragedies, and conflicts of this world is an invisible hierarchy of evil. And some of these invisible rulers are assigned to certain nations and have authority over certain kingdoms of this world.

An evil angel had authority over the kingdom of Persia, and that demon-prince opposed and withstood the angel who had been sent to Daniel, holding God's angel in check for twenty-one days. We don't know how this demon opposed the angel, but the angel tells us that Michael, the chief prince (you might say that he is the "chairman of the joint chiefs of staff" of heaven), came to help this angel. With the added help of Michael, this angel was able to overcome the opposition from the prince of Persia and was able to bring Daniel the answer to his prayer. All of this was happening invisibly behind the scenes of history although Daniel knew nothing of these events.

Is there a demon assigned to the United States of America on a mission to disrupt faith, destroy religious liberty, wage war against the innocent and the unborn, undermine education, destroy truth, embolden evil, ridicule righteousness, pervert justice, and discredit the gospel of Jesus Christ? As you look around at events in our society, doesn't it seem obvious? In fact, the evil "prince of America" has undoubtedly won several promotions for his successful activity in recent years.

And, of course, there is a prince of Russia, a prince of Communist China, a prince of North Korea, a prince of Cuba. It may well be that the prince of modern Iran is the very same prince who invisibly ruled that land when it was called Persia. And perhaps the prince of Babylon is now the prince of Iraq. We can easily see the actions of demonic princes in such historically oppressive nations as Egypt, Saudi Arabia, Afghanistan, Syria, and Libya. We may cheer the overthrow of such human dictators as Hitler, Mussolini, or more recently, Saddam Hussein and Muammar Gaddafi—but the invisible princes continue to rule and oppose God in these nations. That is the revelation the angel showed to Daniel.

Delays can occur in prayer. The next time your prayers are not answered as quickly as you think they should be, remember that you are engaged in spiritual warfare. God's ultimate victory is never in doubt—and God is never too late. He will always provide the resources that are needed for a breakthrough and a victory, as long as faith remains. That's why prayer is so important. The New Testament tells us to pray for those in authority and power so that we might lead peaceable and godly lives (see 1 Timothy 2:1–2). If you believe in the power of prayer and the reality of spiritual warfare, then you should take this biblical counsel to heart. Pray for your leaders. Pray that they will be ruled by God and not by the invisible princes of this world.

PEACE, STRENGTH, AND COURAGE

Next, Daniel tells us about the intense physical effect his vision had upon him. Already weakened by three weeks of fasting and mourning, Daniel found the profound weight of this vision too much to bear:

> While he was saying this to me, I bowed with my face toward the ground and was speechless. Then one who looked like a man touched my lips, and I opened my mouth and began to speak. I said to the one standing before me, "I am overcome with anguish because of the vision, my lord, and I feel very weak. How can I, your servant, talk with you, my lord? My strength is gone and I can hardly breathe." (Daniel 10:15–17)

This tremendous vision was so emotionally and spiritually overwhelming that it simply drained him of physical strength. When we struggle in the spirit, we often pay a physical price. That's why many Christians have such a poor track record of prayer. Authentic prayer is not an easy thing. In fact, it is sometimes an agony to pray.

Paul, writing to the Romans, said, "I urge you, brothers and sisters, by our Lord Jesus Christ and by the love of the Spirit, to join me in my struggle by praying to God for me" (Romans 15:30). A more accurate translation of that last phrase might be, "join me in earnest struggling in prayer to God on my behalf." In the original Greek, it is clear that the struggle Paul refers to is in prayer itself. Authentic prayer is a struggle, and it does take a toll on us—just as it took a toll on Daniel.

As parents, we need to agonize in prayer over our children. As leaders, we need to agonize in prayer over those we lead. As believers, we need to agonize in prayer over those who are lost without the knowledge of Jesus and His good news.

In the final scene, the angel ministers to Daniel in his weakened condition. Daniel writes:

> Again the one who looked like a man touched me and gave me strength. "Do not be afraid, you who are highly esteemed," he said. "Peace! Be strong now; be strong."
>
> When he spoke to me, I was strengthened and said, "Speak, my lord, since you have given me strength." (Daniel 10:18–19)

After the angel's second touch, Daniel felt greatly strengthened. The angel said to him, "Do not be afraid." Why? Because all cause for fear had been removed. The angel went on to say, "Peace! Be strong now; be strong." In other words, peace be with you, be physically strengthened, and be of good courage. The double use of the Hebrew word *chazaq* in the phrase, "Be strong now; be strong," probably signifies a double meaning. This word can mean "be strong" or "be courageous," and it is likely that the angel intends that Daniel be both strengthened and encouraged. When we wrestle and agonize in prayer, God responds by bringing peace to the soul, strength to the body, and courage to the spirit. He ministers to the whole human being.

As Paul wrote to the Christians in Philippi, "Do not be anxious about anything, but in every situation, by prayer and petition, with thanksgiving, present your requests to God. And the peace of God, which transcends all understanding, will guard your hearts and your minds in Christ Jesus" (Philippians 4:6–7). Peace! The peace of God is that wonderful sense that everything will be all right, even though our circumstances say otherwise. It is the sense that God is in control even though everything in our lives seems out of control.

Even though the world is collapsing all around you, you can

have peace in your heart. Moreover, you can have strength in your body and courage in your spirit, just as Daniel had. When the heart is at peace, the body is strengthened. And that, in turn, gives courage to your spirit. The combination of peace, strength, and courage enables you to get up, take up your sword and shield, and rush into the battle again. That is what prayer accomplishes for you.

THE BOOK OF TRUTH

Next, the angel gives Daniel yet another glimpse into the battles that are being fought in the invisible realm of spiritual reality. Daniel writes:

> So he said, "Do you know why I have come to you? Soon I will return to fight against the prince of Persia, and when I go, the prince of Greece will come; but first I will tell you what is written in the Book of Truth. (No one supports me against them except Michael, your prince.)" (Daniel 10:20–21)

The angel says, in effect, "I've got a lot more fighting to do, Daniel, and I have come to strengthen you, so that you might fight alongside me. I'm going back to wage war against the prince of Persia, the invisible angel behind the scenes of Persian affairs. And when I am finished with him, then the prince of Greece will attack. But I have strengthened you, Daniel, so that you might stand with me in all this."

Moreover, the angel said he would tell Daniel what is inscribed in "the Book of Truth." These words serve as an introduction to Daniel 11 and 12, which contain the greatest of all of Daniel's visions. In those chapters, God will unfold to Daniel many amazing events, from Daniel's day to the first appearance of the Lord Jesus then to the end times, which still lie in our own future. In a vivid passage, Daniel sees a vision of the end of this age just before the return of Jesus Christ.

All of this is contained in what the angel calls "the Book of Truth." What an amazing promise the angel gave to Daniel! It reminds us of the promise Jesus gave to His disciples when He said, "But when he, the Spirit of truth, comes, he will guide you into all the truth. He will not speak on his own; he will speak only what he hears, and he will tell you what is yet to come" (John 16:13).

There is only one way we can know what is going to happen in the future and that is to read what is written in the Book of Truth. It is the book God has given us, the book that understands us, the book that knows who we are and how we think. As we open the Book of Truth, and as the Holy Spirit opens our understanding to what is written in that book, we will discover God's program—and we will know how to make ourselves available to Him, so that He can accomplish His agenda through us.

And it all begins with the power of prayer.

9

THE TIME OF THE END

Daniel 11

For decades, self-styled "prophets" and "seers" have predicted that California would be shaken by an earthquake and would sink like mythical Atlantis into the sea. Edgar Cayce predicted it would happen during a window of time between 1958 and 1998. Another supposed "prophet" claimed that volcanoes and "super-mega quakes" would destroy California no later than 1993. Jeane Dixon predicted that a comet would strike one of earth's oceans sometime in the mid-1980s, causing much of the world, including America, to be inundated. Another "prophetess" claimed that because of a gigantic meteor strike not just California but all the western states would soon vanish beneath the waves—and Denver, the mile-high city, would become a seaport.

Self-professed prophets come and go, but California is still here. There are many predictions of great earthquakes in the Bible, but to my knowledge there are no Bible prophecies that specify that California will be the next Atlantis. Earthquake predictions aside, Daniel 11 does contain a great prophecy of cataclysmic events—a prophecy delivered to the prophet Daniel by the angel Gabriel.

As we have already noted, Daniel 10 through 12 comprise one great vision. Up to this point, the chapter divisions in Daniel have divided several distinct prophetic visions or episodes. But the last three chapters of Daniel span a single prophetic vision. So let's not be confused by the chapter divisions.

We saw the background of this vision in Daniel 10. There, Daniel was permitted to look behind the scenes of visible reality and witness the invisible operation of prayer. The moment the curtain was dropped, Daniel beheld a shattering, dazzling sight—a vision of the Lord Jesus Christ in the fullness of His majesty and glory. The impact of this vision was so overwhelming that Daniel was drained of physical and emotional strength. He fell on his face, and an angel came to help him and deliver a detailed vision of prophetic events.

Now, in Daniel 11, the angel unfolds the history of the future from Daniel's era to our own future. Daniel 11 divides into four unequal parts.

Part 1: The Kings of Persia, Verses 1–4
Part 2: Two Kingdoms, Egypt and Syria, Verses 5–20
Part 3: Antiochus Epiphanes, Verses 21–31
Part 4: The Maccabees, Verses 32–35

Let's examine these four sections of Daniel 11 and see what the angel of God revealed to the prophet.

PART 1: THE KINGS OF PERSIA

The first words we read in Daniel 11 actually continue the angel's dialogue from the last verse in Daniel 10. When Daniel wrote this prophecy, it was not divided into chapters and verses. The chapter and verse divisions were added much later, and while God's Word is inspired, these divisions are not.

The division between Daniel 10 and 11 comes at an unfortunate place, interrupting what the angel is saying to Daniel. I will include the last section of Daniel 10 along with the first section of Daniel 11:

> So he [the angel] said, "Do you know why I have come
> to you? Soon I will return to fight against the prince of
> Persia, and when I go, the prince of Greece will come; but
> first I will tell you what is written in the Book of Truth.
> (No one supports me against them except Michael, your
> prince. And in the first year of Darius the Mede, I took
> my stand to support and protect him.)" (Daniel 10:20–
> 11:1)

So the angel explains to Daniel that he has come to do battle
against the "prince" who invisibly rules the nation of Persia. And
later, after this angel leaves Daniel, he will go to do battle against
another "prince," the ruler of Greece. These are not human rulers,
but demons who work behind the scenes of history, waging spiritual
warfare in the invisible heavenly realm, manipulating events in these
nations for the purposes of Satan. This angel tells Daniel that his only
ally in the battle against the demon-princes of Persia and Greece is
the archangel Michael, "your prince." In other words, Michael is the
angelic prince who guards the people and the nation of Israel.

The angel also says that in the first year of the reign of Darius the
Mede, the angel stood against the prince of Persia to protect Darius.
Who was Darius the Mede? We first meet him in Daniel 6, the story
of Daniel's ordeal in the lions' den. Darius is probably the man's
title, not his name, because Darius is an English transliteration of the
Persian word for *rich* or *royal*. Some historians believe that Darius the
Mede was in fact Cyrus the Great (Cyrus II) of Persia. We learned
in Daniel 6 that Darius the Mede was quite fond of his prime minister, Daniel. For Daniel's sake, Darius was kindly disposed toward
the people of Israel. (When Darius sent Daniel to the lions' den, it
was not because he was angry with Daniel but because he had been
tricked and maneuvered into doing so by Daniel's enemies.)

Why did the angel take a stand to support and protect Darius the
Mede? It's because Darius protected the people of Israel during their
exile in Babylon. God always blesses the individuals and nations that

bless and defend the Jewish people. This is a principle that God set forth in His promise to Abraham, the father of the Jewish people:

> "I will make you into a great nation,
>   and I will bless you;
> I will make your name great,
>   and you will be a blessing.
> I will bless those who bless you,
>   and whoever curses you I will curse;
> and all peoples on earth
>   will be blessed through you." (Genesis 12:2–3)

Satan has always been at work to destroy the Hebrew people. The Jews have always had to struggle for survival. In ancient times the Hebrews battled the Canaanite tribes who tried to destroy them. The Jews were conquered and exiled by the Babylonians, slaughtered and dispersed by the Romans, suffered persecution and pogroms in the Middle Ages, and survived the Nazi Holocaust of World War II. The Jewish people and the state of Israel still endure the hatred of a hostile world today. It is Satan and his demon princes who stir up this murderous intent against God's chosen people—but God has given Israel a great defender, the archangel Michael.

While giving Daniel this glimpse into the warfare that is being waged in the spiritual realm, the angel goes on to say, "I will tell you what is written in the Book of Truth." With these words, he introduces a grand tour of future history, beginning with the time of the Persian kings:

> "Now then, I tell you the truth: Three more kings will arise in Persia, and then a fourth, who will be far richer than all the others. When he has gained power by his wealth, he will stir up everyone against the kingdom of Greece. Then a mighty king will arise, who will rule with great power and do as he pleases. After he has arisen, his

empire will be broken up and parceled out toward the
four winds of heaven. It will not go to his descendants,
nor will it have the power he exercised, because his empire
will be uprooted and given to others." (Daniel 11:2–4)

The opening verses of this prophecy cover a span of approximately ninety-five years. Do you recognize the historic personalities that appear in this prediction? The angel tells Daniel that three more kings will follow Darius the Mede (who is probably Cyrus the Great). These three Persian kings are known to history.

The first was Cambyses, the son of Cyrus. He was overthrown by a usurper who took the name of Cambyses' son, Smerdis, and is known by historians as Pseudo-Smerdis ("false-Smerdis"). The third king was Darius Hystaspes. If you have studied ancient Persian history in school, you will recognize this name. Also called Darius the Great, Darius Hystaspes ruled the Persian Empire at the height of its power, when the empire reached from the Balkans and Greece in the west to Central Asia and Pakistan in the east, and as far into Africa as Egypt, Libya, and Sudan.

The angel says that a fourth king would follow. This does not mean that he would be the last king of Persia, but that he would be the fourth king from Daniel's day. Moreover, this fourth king would be especially notable.

The fourth king in this prophecy was Xerxes the Great, king of Persia, who was indeed fabulously rich, as the angel told Daniel. He became strong through his riches—and when Xerxes flexed his power, he stirred up the antagonism of the kingdom of Greece. The Persians under Xerxes conducted raids against the Greeks, which inflamed Greek passions and motivated Alexander the Great to go to war against the Persians.

The angel goes on to say, "Then a mighty king will arise, who will rule with great power and do as he pleases. After he has arisen, his empire will be broken up and parceled out toward the four winds of heaven." This "mighty king" is clearly Alexander the Great, the young warrior who became first king of Macedon and then king of Greece. He led the Greek armies against the Persian Empire, overthrew the might of Persia, and swept on to conquer the civilized world of that time.

According to the angel's prophecy, Alexander was to be "broken" and his empire "parceled out toward the four winds of heaven." Alexander died at age thirty-two, and his kingdom was divided, but not to his posterity. At the time of Alexander's death he had an unborn son who did briefly inherit the kingdom. But the empire was ultimately divided among the Diadochi ("Successors"), principally his four top generals. For a king, having his kingdom divided up among four generals instead of being passed down to an heir was the equivalent of the kingdom being broken up and scattered to "the four winds of heaven." The angel also said that this king's empire would be "uprooted and given to others"—a hint of the fact that the fragments of the shattered Greek Empire would later be conquered by the Romans from the West.

PART 2: TWO KINGDOMS, EGYPT AND SYRIA

The next section of the vision encompasses verses 5–20. The angel traces the course of two empires, one to the south of Israel and one to the north. The king of the south is Egypt under Ptolemy (one of the generals of Alexander) and his successors. The king of the north is Syria. That domain was under the rule of the Seleucids (Seleucus was another of Alexander's generals).

> "The king of the South will become strong, but one of his commanders will become even stronger than he and will rule his own kingdom with great power. After some years, they will become allies. The daughter of the king of the South will go to the king of the North to make an alliance, but she will not retain her power, and he and his power will not last. In those days she will be betrayed,

together with her royal escort and her father and the one who supported her.

"One from her family line will arise to take her place. He will attack the forces of the king of the North and enter his fortress; he will fight against them and be victorious. He will also seize their gods, their metal images and their valuable articles of silver and gold and carry them off to Egypt. For some years he will leave the king of the North alone. Then the king of the North will invade the realm of the king of the South but will retreat to his own country. His sons will prepare for war and assemble a great army, which will sweep on like an irresistible flood and carry the battle as far as his fortress.

"Then the king of the South will march out in a rage and fight against the king of the North, who will raise a large army, but it will be defeated. When the army is carried off, the king of the South will be filled with pride and will slaughter many thousands, yet he will not remain triumphant. For the king of the North will muster another army, larger than the first; and after several years, he will advance with a huge army fully equipped.

"In those times many will rise against the king of the South. Those who are violent among your own people will rebel in fulfillment of the vision, but without success. Then the king of the North will come and build up siege ramps and will capture a fortified city. The forces of the South will be powerless to resist; even their best troops will not have the strength to stand. The invader will do as he pleases; no one will be able to stand against him. He will establish himself in the Beautiful Land and will have the power to destroy it. He will determine to come with the might of his entire kingdom and will make an alliance with the king of the South. And he will give him a daughter in marriage in order to overthrow the kingdom, but his plans will not succeed or help him. Then he will turn his attention to the coastlands and will take many of them, but a commander will put an end to his insolence and will turn his insolence back on him. After this, he will turn back toward the fortresses of his own country but will stumble and fall, to be seen no more.

"His successor will send out a tax collector to maintain the royal splendor. In a few years, however, he will be destroyed, yet not in anger or in battle." (Daniel 11:5–20)

These two kingdoms, Egypt and Syria, fought back and forth over the course of about a hundred thirty years. Poor Israel was caught between the two warring kingdoms and often became the battlefield where these armies waged their wars. Jerusalem was captured repeatedly by one side or the other, and was sacked and ravaged many times. The city and its people were continually ground like wheat between two millstones during this conflict between the kings to the north and the south.

The account of these kingdoms is given to us because of Israel's involvement. God's primary concern is for Israel, so for her sake He gives us this detailed account, which history has confirmed in every detail.

PART 3: ANTIOCHUS EPIPHANES

Next, the angel tells Daniel of a coming king of the North. History knows this king as Antiochus Epiphanes. We met him earlier in Daniel 8. He is the "little horn" who persecuted Israel and set up the first "abomination of desolation" in the temple at Jerusalem. He has been called "The Antichrist of the Old Testament," a most despicable character, yet a remarkable man in many ways. He reigned from 175 to 164 BC. Originally named Mithridates, he gave himself the name Antiochus Epiphanes—"God Manifest"—and he named his capital city, Antioch, after himself.

There are certain highlights of this prophetic passage worth noting, because they have a bearing on the times in which we live today: Here's what the angel said to Daniel:

> "He will be succeeded by a contemptible person who has not been given the honor of royalty. He will invade the kingdom when its people feel secure, and he will seize it through intrigue. Then an overwhelming army will be swept away before him; both it and a prince of the covenant will be destroyed. After coming to an agreement with him, he will act deceitfully, and with only a few people he will rise to power. When the richest provinces feel secure, he will invade them and will achieve what neither his fathers nor his forefathers did. He will distribute plunder, loot and wealth among his followers. He will plot the overthrow of fortresses—but only for a time.
>
> "With a large army he will stir up his strength and courage against the king of the South. The king of the South will wage war with a large and very powerful army, but he will not be able to stand because of the plots devised against him. Those who eat from the king's provisions will try to destroy him; his army will be swept away, and many will fall in battle. The two kings, with their hearts bent on evil, will sit at the same table and lie to each other, but to no avail, because an end will still come at the appointed time. The king of the North will return to his own country with great wealth, but his heart will be set against the holy covenant. He will take action against it and then return to his own country."
> (Daniel 11:21–28)

The angel told Daniel how this treacherous man, Antiochus Epiphanes, would come to power. Once in power, he would launch—and win—a military campaign against Egypt. This victory would enhance his power and position. The angel goes on to tell us what would happen next:

> "At the appointed time he will invade the South again, but this time the outcome will be different from what it was before. Ships of the western coastlands will oppose him, and he will lose heart. Then he will turn back and vent his fury against the holy covenant. He will return and show favor to those who forsake the holy covenant."
> (Daniel 11:29–30)

History records that Antiochus made a second invasion of Egypt—but this time he met with difficulty. He led his army into Egypt, but the Egyptians sent for help from the Romans. The Roman Senate sent a general named Popilius, who led a legion against Antiochus. They arrived in Roman galleys, which are referred to here as "ships of the western coastlands."

Popilius insisted that Antiochus return to his own land, keep the peace, and acknowledge the authority of Rome. Antiochus asked for time to consider these terms, but Popilius drew a circle around him with his sword and told him to decide before he stepped out of that circle. So Antiochus gave in and promised to keep the peace. But instead of honoring his promise to Popilius, Antiochus did what the angel prophesied in the next verse:

> "His armed forces will rise up to desecrate the temple fortress and will abolish the daily sacrifice. Then they will set up the abomination that causes desolation."
> (Daniel 11:31)

At around the same time, there was an insurrection in Jerusalem, and the false high priest whom Antiochus had installed in the temple in Jerusalem was forced to flee. Stinging from his humiliation at the hands of the Romans and further enraged by the rebellion in

Jerusalem, Antiochus attacked the city, slaughtered forty thousand men, women, and children, and he sold an additional forty thousand people into slavery. He banned the Hebrew religion, forced the Jews to sacrifice to idols, and tortured and executed anyone who kept the Sabbath or honored the Scriptures.

Antiochus set up "the rebellion that causes desolation" in the temple, sacrificing a pig to Zeus, then sprinkling the blood and juices of the pig around the sanctuary to defile the temple. Then he set up an idol of Zeus in the holy place. All this is important to us today because it was a preview of an even more blasphemous abomination of desolation that is yet to come.

PART 4: THE MACCABEES

In the next section, the angel describes a band of remarkable people known as the Maccabees. They were an army of Hebrew rebels who wrested control of Judea from the Seleucid Empire of Antiochus Epiphanes. The Maccabees founded the Hasmonean Dynasty, reestablished the Hebrew sacrifices, and destroyed idols and other symbols of Greek (Hellenistic) influence in Judea.

The Maccabean revolt was ignited when a Jewish priest named Mattathias refused to worship the Greek gods set up in Jerusalem by Antiochus Epiphanes. Mattathias killed a Hellenistic Jew who was sacrificing to the Greek gods, then he and his five sons fled into the wilderness. There they raised up an army to fight a guerilla war against their Seleucid oppressors. After the death of Mattathias, his son Judah Maccabee led the resistance. (The name "Maccabee" is believed to derive from the Aramaic *maqqaba*, meaning "hammer," in recognition of Judah's ferocity in battle.)

The revolt succeeded. The Maccabees recaptured the temple, cleansed the sanctuary, and restored the Jewish sacrifices. The Jewish feast of Hanukkah (meaning "Dedication") recalls the restoration of Jewish worship on the 25th of Kislev (December 14) 164 BC after Judah Maccabee and his army removed the Greek idols from the temple. Here is what the angel tells Daniel about Antiochus Epiphanes and the revolt of the Maccabees:

> "With flattery he will corrupt those who have violated the covenant, but the people who know their God will firmly resist him.
>
> "Those who are wise will instruct many, though for a time they will fall by the sword or be burned or captured or plundered. When they fall, they will receive a little help, and many who are not sincere will join them. Some of the wise will stumble, so that they may be refined, purified and made spotless until the time of the end, for it will still come at the appointed time." (Daniel 11:32–35)

This is a remarkable prophecy. This passage contains such a detailed description of the corrupt rule of Antiochus Epiphanes and the valiant resistance of the Maccabees that many Bible critics have concluded that the book of Daniel had to have been written after these events took place. But as we saw in chapter 2, ancient manuscripts found among the Dead Sea Scrolls, combined with other archaeological and textual evidence, make it clear that the book of Daniel must have been written around 600 BC.

The prophecy the angel gave to Daniel predicts the rise of a people who would know their God, would instruct many, and would perform daring exploits in battle. Yet they would receive little help and would ultimately be overcome. The Maccabees had to appeal to the Romans for help, and this appeal ultimately led to Roman control over Palestine. The Romans still ruled Palestine when our Lord was born.

While they were in power, the Maccabees were zealous for God and did great works in His name, just as the angel predicted. The Maccabees cleansed the temple sanctuary and restored the sacrificial offerings of the Jews. And in the end—also as predicted—the Maccabees fell by the sword and flame, by captivity and plunder.

The angel makes a strange statement in verse 35: "Some of the wise will stumble, so that they may be refined, purified and made spotless until the time of the end, for it will still come at the appointed time." Note that reference to "the time of the end." This seems to suggest a fast-forward from the time of the Maccabees to the time we call the last days. Clearly, this prophecy of the Maccabean resistance against Antiochus Epiphanes appears to have a double fulfillment—and the later fulfillment will be a greater fulfillment. It will take place in the last days, in a time yet to be appointed.

THE KING WHO EXALTS HIMSELF

Now we come to the last section of the chapter. In these verses, we see an Old Testament picture of the person who is pictured in the book of Revelation as "the second beast" and "the false prophet":

> "The king will do as he pleases. He will exalt and magnify himself above every god and will say unheard-of things against the God of gods. He will be successful until the time of wrath is completed, for what has been determined must take place. He will show no regard for the gods of his ancestors or for the one desired by women, nor will he regard any god, but will exalt himself above them all. Instead of them, he will honor a god of fortresses; a god unknown to his ancestors he will honor with gold and silver, with precious stones and costly gifts. He will attack the mightiest fortresses with the help of a foreign god and will greatly honor those who acknowledge him. He will make them rulers over many people and will distribute the land at a price.
>
> "At the time of the end the king of the South will engage him in battle, and the king of the North will storm out against him with chariots and cavalry and a great fleet of ships. He will invade many countries and

sweep through them like a flood. He will also invade the Beautiful Land. Many countries will fall, but Edom, Moab and the leaders of Ammon will be delivered from his hand. He will extend his power over many countries; Egypt will not escape. He will gain control of the treasures of gold and silver and all the riches of Egypt, with the Libyans and Cushites in submission. But reports from the east and the north will alarm him, and he will set out in a great rage to destroy and annihilate many. He will pitch his royal tents between the seas at the beautiful holy mountain. Yet he will come to his end, and no one will help him." (Daniel 11:36–45)

This false prophet is accepted by the Jews as the Messiah, and he erects the abomination of desolation for a final time in the temple in Jerusalem—a temple that has not yet been rebuilt. God's prophetic word is sure, and the temple will exist in the last days.

This is yet another prophecy requiring double fulfillment. It was fulfilled in the days of Antiochus Epiphanes and the Maccabees, and it will be fulfilled again (and more profoundly) in the last days, at the appointed time. These are significant prophetic insights that may well affect our lives in profound ways.

In order for this prophecy to be fulfilled in our own future, Egypt (the kingdom of the South) and Syria (the kingdom of the North) will have to be enemies instead of allies. Egypt and Syria were once part of the same nation, the United Arab Republic (UAR). But that union, based largely on their shared hatred of Israel, lasted only from 1958 to 1961, when Syria seceded from the UAR. Today, Egypt and Syria are divided on many issues—and it will be a profoundly important sign of the times when these two nations are at odds.

The person referred to in Daniel 11 as "the king of the North," the king who "will exalt and magnify himself above every god and will say unheard-of things against the God of gods," is the same person who is referred to in the book of Revelation as "the second beast" and "the false prophet." In Revelation 13, John writes about two beasts.

In Revelation 13:1, John writes, "And I saw a beast coming out of the sea." This is the leader of the Western confederacy of nations, the iron kingdom descended from the Roman Empire. This is the person we generally refer to as the Antichrist (although the term "Antichrist" never appears in either Daniel or Revelation; that term only appears in 1 and 2 John).

Then in Revelation 13:11, John writes, "Then I saw a second beast, coming out of the earth." This second beast is the false prophet (see Revelation 16:13; 19:20; 20:10). Whereas the first beast, the Antichrist, came out of the sea (and the Antichrist would come from across the sea), the second beast would come from nearby, from out of the earth, from Syria, just north of Israel. This second beast will exercise authority in the name of the first beast, will make the people of the earth worship the first beast, will perform signs and wonders, will deceive the world, and will force everyone in the world to receive the mark of the beast.

This second beast, the false prophet, is the person described as "the king of the North" in Daniel 11. He is the king who will exalt himself. And he is the king who will set up an image of the first beast, the Western political leader, in the temple—the ultimate abomination of desolation. If we look ahead to Daniel 12:1, we will see a confirmation that this prophecy deals not only with the time of Antiochus Epiphanes but also with the last days. There, the angel tells Daniel:

> "At that time Michael, the great prince who protects your people, will arise. There will be a time of distress such as has not happened from the beginning of nations until then." (Daniel 12:1)

This "time of trouble" is clearly the great tribulation that our Lord speaks of in Matthew 24. So there is no question that this passage in Daniel 11 deals with the last days. Notice another statement by the angel to Daniel in chapter 12:

> "From the time that the daily sacrifice is abolished and the abomination that causes desolation is set up, there will be 1,290 days. Blessed is the one who waits for and reaches the end of the 1,335 days." (Daniel 12:11–12)

This refers to the last desecration of the temple that is to occur, and it refers back to this verse in Daniel 11, describing the desecration under Antiochus Epiphanes:

> "His armed forces will rise up to desecrate the temple fortress and will abolish the daily sacrifice. Then they will set up the abomination that causes desolation." (Daniel 11:31)

So it appears certain that this vision is subject to a double interpretation and a double fulfillment. It was fulfilled in the time of Antiochus Epiphanes, and this vision—particularly from verses 21 through 45—will be even more profoundly and globally fulfilled in the future, at the appointed time in the last days.

SETTLING THE ANCIENT QUARREL

Now let's zoom in for a closer look at this king of the North, the false prophet, and his impact on the closing days of history. There are several aspects of this person that we should note.

The angel tells Daniel that this king, the false prophet, is a blasphemer. The false prophet will exalt himself above all religions, all gods, including the one true God. Blasphemy is always the mark of the spirit of antichrist.

The false prophet is also supremely arrogant and narcissistic. This does not mean that he will be recognized as arrogant by other people. In fact, he will probably project an image of being very humble. Narcissistic people often create an image of themselves to hide who they really are inside. Daniel 8 tells us that the false prophet exalts himself "in his own mind," not openly, and that he is a master of deception: "By his cunning he shall make deceit prosper under his hand, and in his own mind he shall magnify himself" (Daniel 8:25, Revised Standard Version; the NIV is not as clear on this point).

The angel reveals that the false prophet "will be successful until the time of wrath is completed" (Daniel 11:36). The phrase "the time of wrath" refers to the great tribulation. It indicates that the false prophet will have power and influence over the entire Middle East and perhaps over much of the world in conjunction with the great Western ruler (the Antichrist) during Daniel's seventieth week—and especially during the final three and a half years, the time of the great tribulation.

We also learn that the false prophet will rule by military power. The angel tells Daniel that this person will "honor a god of fortresses; a god unknown to his ancestors he will honor with gold and silver, with precious stones and costly gifts. He will attack the mightiest fortresses with the help of a foreign god and will greatly honor those who acknowledge him. He will make them rulers over many people and will distribute the land at a price" (11:38–39).

This "king of the North," the false prophet, is a religious leader, a political leader, and a military leader. He is backed by an enormous military power—and in Revelation 13 we see that the source of his military power is his alliance with the leader of the Western world, the last Caesar, the Antichrist. The restored Roman Empire will be dominant in the last days, and the false prophet will cause the whole world to worship the leader of that empire, the Antichrist.

The king of the North, the Syrian king, will be in league with a foreign god—"a god of fortresses; a god unknown to his ancestors"—and this foreign god is the Western leader, the first beast of Revelation 13. The dominant religion of the world in that day will be the worship of one man, the great Antichrist of the last days. The

Syrian king of the North will lead the world in the worship of the Western leader, the Antichrist.

The angel tells Daniel that the false prophet "will distribute the land at a price." This suggests the possibility that the false prophet will finally settle the ancient quarrel between Arabs and Jews over ownership of the land of Israel. Today, this quarrel divides the Middle East, and indeed the whole world. Until this problem is settled, there can be no hope for peace. In the last days, the false prophet will succeed in bringing peace to this region—but only for a limited time.

THE KING OF THE SOUTH

The climactic war of the last days is described in the closing section of Daniel 11. The angel tells Daniel that at "the time of the end"—during the great tribulation, in the middle of Daniel's seventieth week—"the king of the South will engage [the king of the North] in battle, and the king of the North will storm out against him with chariots and cavalry and a great fleet of ships. He will invade many countries and sweep through them like a flood. He will also invade the Beautiful Land" (vv. 40–41). The "Beautiful Land," of course, refers to Israel.

This great war begins when Syria (the king of the North) attacks Egypt (the king of the South). Their ancient hatred for each other is reignited, and Israel once again becomes a convenient battlefield for these two warring forces. What triggers the war between Syria and Egypt? This hostility undoubtedly arises because the false prophet, the king of the North, has made a covenant with the Jewish state, the nation of Israel. The false prophet has permitted the Jews to rebuild the temple in Jerusalem and restore Jewish worship and sacrifices. This covenant angers the Egyptians.

So, during these times of rising tension, hatred, and hostility, the king of the South, Egypt, attacks and engages the king of the North, Syria, in battle. In reply, the king of the North storms out against the Egyptian forces with "chariots and cavalry and a great fleet of ships." Undoubtedly, the chariots and cavalry and ships will be of the most modern design, and they will deliver death and horror on a scale the human race has never witnessed before.

Where would the relatively small nation of Syria obtain such firepower in today's world? In recent decades, Syria has been closely aligned with (and heavily rearmed by) Russia. It's very likely that when this war is fought, it will be fought in large part with Russian-made weapons.

The false prophet will conquer a number of countries including Ammon (modern-day Jordan), and he "will extend his power over many countries; Egypt will not escape. He will gain control of the treasures of gold and silver and all the riches of Egypt, with the Libyans and Cushites in submission" (Daniel 11:42–43). His forces will conquer Egypt (the king of the South), plus other nations across North Africa.

To reach Egypt and North Africa, the king of the North will have to come down through Palestine—that is, through Israel. Perhaps it is at this time that the false prophet sets up the abomination of desolation in the temple. In any case, the false prophet's forces sweep down through Egypt, conquering the nations of North Africa. But even as the false prophet is savoring this triumph, disaster strikes. He hears alarming reports from the east and the north—from the direction of Israel and Syria, and even further east and north, from Russia or even China. The book of Revelation makes a cryptic reference to a vast eastern army that has gathered at the banks of the River Euphrates:

> The number of the mounted troops was twice ten thousand times ten thousand. I heard their number. (Revelation 9:16)

That figure, "twice ten thousand times ten thousand," is 200 million soldiers. Who commands them? Later in the book of Revelation, we learn:

> The sixth angel poured out his bowl on the great river
> Euphrates, and its water was dried up to prepare the way
> for the kings from the East. (Revelation 16:12)

These 200 million soldiers are commanded by "kings from the East," or literally "kings of the sun-rising." Currently, the only nation that could put 200 million soldiers in uniform is Communist China.

So it appears likely that while the king of the North (the false prophet) is occupied in North Africa, the kings from the East decide to take military advantage of the situation. When the king of the North learns of this, he is alarmed, as the angel tells Daniel: "But tidings from the east and the north shall alarm him, and he shall go forth with great fury to exterminate and utterly destroy many. And he shall pitch his palatial tents between the sea and the glorious holy mountain; yet he shall come to his end, with none to help him" (11:44–45 RSV). This passage describes what the book of Revelation calls the Battle of Armageddon.

The king of the North is alarmed because he is down in Egypt, his supply line is stretched thin—and he learns that a force of 200 million men is coming from the East with plans to cut his supply line. The angel tells Daniel what the king of the North does next: "He will pitch his royal tents between the seas at the beautiful holy mountain. Yet he will come to his end, and no one will help him."

The false prophet hurriedly moves his forces into the land of Israel, making his camp in the plains between the Mediterranean and the holy mountain of Jerusalem. There he will make his last stand—and he will be alone. His allies will not come to his aid. The book of Revelation describes the end of the false prophet, the king of the North, along with the Antichrist, when the Lord Jesus returns at the end of the age:

> I saw heaven standing open and there before me was a
> white horse, whose rider is called Faithful and True. With

justice he judges and wages war. His eyes are like blazing fire, and on his head are many crowns. He has a name written on him that no one knows but he himself. He is dressed in a robe dipped in blood, and his name is the Word of God. The armies of heaven were following him, riding on white horses and dressed in fine linen, white and clean. Coming out of his mouth is a sharp sword with which to strike down the nations. "He will rule them with an iron scepter." He treads the winepress of the fury of the wrath of God Almighty. On his robe and on his thigh he has this name written:

KING OF KINGS AND LORD OF LORDS.

And I saw an angel standing in the sun, who cried in a loud voice to all the birds flying in midair, "Come, gather together for the great supper of God, so that you may eat the flesh of kings, generals, and the mighty, of horses and their riders, and the flesh of all people, free and slave, great and small."

Then I saw the beast and the kings of the earth and their armies gathered together to wage war against the rider on the horse and his army. But the beast was captured, and with it the false prophet who had performed the signs on its behalf. With these signs he had deluded those who had received the mark of the beast and worshiped its image. The two of them were thrown alive into the fiery lake of burning sulfur. The rest were killed with the sword coming out of the mouth of the rider on the horse, and all the birds gorged themselves on their flesh. (Revelation 19:11–21)

This narrative in the book of Revelation fills in a lot of details for us regarding the defeat and destruction of the king of the North, the false prophet. All of this is summed up by the angel when he tells Daniel, "Yet he will come to his end, and no one will help him" (Daniel 11:45). The lawless one, the king who exalted himself, will be brought to a final end by the glorious appearing of the Lord Jesus Christ in His power and glory. As we have seen throughout the book of Daniel, the kingdoms of this world will become the kingdom of our Lord, and of His Christ, and He shall reign forever.

DON'T BE AFRAID

Many people, when they contemplate these predictive passages of Scripture, are inclined to be afraid of the future. But God has not given us these prophecies to frighten us. He didn't intend that we should go out and dig bomb shelters and hide ourselves in the ground. Nor did He intend that we sell all our possessions and go up on a mountaintop and wait for Christ to return, as various "doomsday cults" have done over the years.

God has given us these prophecies for a sound, practical reason. He is preparing us so that we will not be deceived by the delusion of the last days. That delusion will involve the worship of a human being, the Antichrist. That is the ultimate delusion, and many people will fall for it.

Humanism, the philosophy that we human beings can become our own god and do not need any other god is the final and ultimate lie of Satan—and it is virtually identical to Satan's original lie in the garden of Eden: You will be like God.

Increasingly, we see men and women falling for that same lie, worshiping at the altar of the self, seeking to be their own god, telling themselves they have no need of the one true God. At the same time, the propaganda mills of our secular culture are churning out books and pamphlets, movies and TV shows, telling us there is no God, we have outgrown our need for God, and we can be our own gods. It's the oldest lie in the book, but it still sells.

UNDERSTAND THE REASONS FOR PROPHECY

God has given us these prophetic passages in Daniel, as well as other parts of the Old and New Testaments, so that we would not be deceived. In fact, I want to suggest four practical reasons why God has given us Bible prophecy:

First, Bible prophecy helps us to have a realistic view of humanity. It shows us the futility of trying to solve our own sin problem, our own fallen condition. Through prophecy, we gain the long view of history, from the beginning to the end, and we learn that there is no humanly devised solution that can ever work. Obviously, this doesn't mean we give up. We still seek to grow spiritually, live compassionately, serve obediently, and alleviate the pain and misery of the people around us. But all of our solutions are temporary at best. We have no illusions that we will ever solve the problems that result from our own fallenness.

We cannot solve the human condition with social programs, by electing this or that political party to office, by passing more stringent laws, by improving education, or by giving people money, food, housing, and other programs. We may be able to alleviate some suffering or improve people's understanding of their situation, but we cannot solve the problem of the human condition. We were born into sin as children of Adam and Eve, and only God can solve that problem—and He solved it through His Son, Jesus. Bible prophecy helps us to understand that this is so. It gives us a realistic view of our human condition.

Second, Bible prophecy teaches us to employ spiritual weapons rather than human strategies and pressure tactics in order to solve human problems. It continually amazes me that Christians do not seem to learn this lesson. Our warfare is spiritual warfare. Our weapons are spiritual weapons: the belt of God's truth, the armor of God's righteousness, the gospel of peace, the shield of faith, the helmet of salvation, the sword of God's Word, and the power of prayer (see Ephesians 6:14–18). Our struggle is not against flesh and blood but against spiritual forces of evil in the invisible realms (see 6:12).

For some reason, we insist on conducting this battle our own way, using human wisdom, human strategy, and human tactics. We would rather establish a program or launch a political campaign or conduct a protest rally than to simply go to God in prayer. We would rather operate in our own wisdom and strength than call upon the omniscience and omnipotence that created the universe. The fact that we neglect our spiritual weapons is proof that we do not believe what our Lord has told us. If we really trusted in the firepower of our spiritual arsenal, we would rely on that power 100 percent.

Third, Bible prophecy teaches us to manifest a spirit of trust in God and confidence in His Word, in spite of the worsening conditions in this world. Many of us, when we hear about the cataclysmic events of the end times, begin to quake in fear. But Jesus said we should have exactly the opposite reaction: "When these things begin to take place, stand up and lift up your heads, because your redemption is drawing near" (Luke 21:28). When we see prophecy being fulfilled, we should not despair—we should rejoice! This means that history is playing out exactly as God said it would. This should confirm our faith, not weaken it.

Fourth, Bible prophecy helps us to build ties of love toward our fellow believers. As the world grows darker, Christian love and fellowship become all the more important to our lives. The writer to the Hebrews wrote, "And let us consider how we may spur one another on toward love and good deeds, not giving up meeting together, as some are in the habit of doing, but encouraging one another—and all the more as you see the Day approaching" (Hebrews 10:24–25).

We need one another in the body of Christ—and that need grows as the end times approach. Don't isolate yourself from other believers or go off on your own. Get to know your brothers and sisters in Christ. Believers need to spend time together, praying together, studying the Word together, encouraging one another, serving one another, loving one another, and learning to trust one another. The day may come when you will be called on to lay down your lives for one another—and you will do so with joyful hearts because these people will have become your family of faith.

Bible prophecy was not given to us to satisfy our curiosity, but to spur us on to obedience, righteousness, and love. It was not given to increase our knowledge but to change our lives. It was given to move us from a mere profession of faith to a deeper practice of faith.

The King of Kings and Lord of Lords is coming to put an end to war and tribulation, to sin and suffering. That is the encouraging, uplifting message of these prophetic passages for your life and mine.

So stand up, brothers and sisters! Lift up your heads, because your redemption is coming soon!

=10=

THE LAST WORD

Daniel 12

I once heard a story about a priest in the Philippines, and while I cannot say for certain that this story is literally true, I know that it contains a great truth. It's the story of a Catholic priest who loved God dearly and served Him faithfully. But deep within his soul, he carried a burden of guilt for a secret sin he had committed many years before, while he was in seminary. Even though he had repented of that sin, he never felt a sense of peace and forgiveness from God.

The priest had in his parish a woman who was said to experience visions in which she spoke face-to-face with Jesus. The priest was skeptical of this claim, so he decided to test her and see if her visions really came from the Lord. He said, "The next time you speak to Jesus in a vision, ask Him what secret sin I committed when I was in seminary."

A few days later, the priest visited the woman and asked, "Did Jesus visit you in your dreams?"

"Yes, He did," she said.

"Did you ask Him what sin I committed in seminary?"

"Yes."

"And what did He tell you?"

"He said, 'I don't remember.'"

All of the visions in the book of Daniel ultimately focus on one truth: The Lord Jesus is coming, and when He comes, He will set people free from the curse of sin, and God will remember our sins no more. It's easy to become focused on the cataclysmic future events in Bible prophecy and to think that the visions of the book of Daniel are about the end of the world. But the true focus of these visions is Christ himself and His redemptive work in your life and mine.

We come to the end of Daniel's great final vision, which occupies Daniel 10 through 12. The first three verses of Daniel 12 contain the conclusion of the vision, which began in Daniel 10 and continued through Daniel 11. After those verses, there is a postscript to the book of Daniel, in which we again meet the man dressed in linen (from Daniel 10), who is Jesus the Lord. This postscript underscores the fact that Jesus, and He alone, is the focus of this prophecy—and indeed of all Bible prophecy.

THE TIME OF JACOB'S TROUBLES

As Daniel 12 opens, the angel is still speaking to Daniel and revealing the concluding images of the vision. Daniel records:

> "At that time Michael, the great prince who protects your people, will arise. There will be a time of distress such as has not happened from the beginning of nations until then. But at that time your people—everyone whose name is found written in the book—will be delivered." (Daniel 12:1)

The phrase "at that time" refers to the time of the events described in the closing verses of Daniel 11. In other words, what happens next in Daniel 12 takes place at the same time that "the king of the North," the false prophet, erects the abomination of desolation, defiling the temple in Jerusalem for the last time.

When those events begin, the archangel Michael, the great angelic prince who defends Daniel's people, Israel, shall arise. He will serve the Jewish people during the time of their greatest distress—a time even more horrifying than the Nazi Holocaust of World War II. Michael will make sure that all those whose names are "written in the book" are delivered safely through those terrible days.

Michael is a fascinating character who appears in the Old Testament only in Daniel 10:13, 21, and 12:1, and in the New Testament in verse 9 of Jude (where he is called the archangel) and Revelation 12:7. In Jude, we read that the archangel Michael disputed with Satan over the body of the departed Moses. We don't know what this dispute involved, but we do know that when Michael opposed Satan, he did so in his role as the defender of God's chosen people. In Revelation, we see Michael leading the angelic hosts of heaven against Satan and his fallen angels when they are cast out of heaven and confined to earth. The defeated Satan, when he is cast down, knows that he has but a short time, and his wrath is terrible.

There is one other reference to Michael the archangel in the New Testament, though he is not referred to by name. The apostle Paul writes of the time when the Lord Jesus comes for His church, the event often referred to as the rapture:

> For the Lord himself will come down from heaven, with a
> loud command, with the voice of the archangel and with
> the trumpet call of God, and the dead in Christ will rise
> first. (1 Thessalonians 4:16)

Since the only archangel mentioned in Scripture is Michael, this helps us to know the order of the events in the last days. When the Lord comes to take His church out of the world, Michael will arrive to stand up and act on behalf of the people he is assigned to protect, Israel. Many Bible scholars believe this means that when the church is removed from the earth, Israel will come into the forefront again as a nation under God. At that point in history, God will begin His renewed program of activity through His people, the Jews.

This accords with what the angel says to Daniel: "At that time Michael, the great prince who protects your people, will arise. There will be a time of distress such as has not happened from the beginning of nations until then" (12:1). It may well be that when Jesus arrives for His church, and His arrival is accompanied by the voice of the archangel, this means that Michael has come to defend Israel as the tribulation begins.

The Lord Jesus speaks of the tribulation in almost identical terms as we see here in Daniel: "For then there will be great distress, unequaled from the beginning of the world until now—and never to be equaled again" (Matthew 24:21). These will be both the worst and the last of Israel's many times of trouble.

Anyone who visits Israel these days cannot help but be impressed with the industriousness of the Jewish nation. They have replanted the land, turning deserts into lush, green, productive farms. They have created highly profitable centers of commerce and manufacturing. The bustling economic activity of the nation of Israel speaks volumes about the hopes of the Jewish people for peace and security within their own borders.

But if you know your Bible, you know that a time of great trial lies ahead for Israel. The Old Testament prophet Jeremiah describes this time:

> These are the words the LORD spoke concerning Israel and Judah: "This is what the LORD says:
>
> "'Cries of fear are heard—
>   terror, not peace.
> Ask and see:
>   Can a man bear children?
> Then why do I see every strong man
>   with his hands on his stomach like a woman
>   in labor,
>   every face turned deathly pale?

> How awful that day will be!
>> No other will be like it.
> It will be a time of trouble for Jacob,
>> but he will be saved out of it.'"
>
> (Jeremiah 30:4–7)

This description of the time of Jacob's troubles agrees with the prophecy of the angel to Daniel. When Michael arises, there shall be a time of unprecedented trouble in Israel, yet "at that time your people—everyone whose name is found written in the book—will be delivered" (Daniel 12:1). A precious remnant, a persecuted minority, will be kept safe during this time of evil and peril.

THE COMING RESURRECTION

The angel goes on to tell Daniel: "Multitudes who sleep in the dust of the earth will awake: some to everlasting life, others to shame and everlasting contempt" (Daniel 12:2).

The Old Testament does not say very much about the resurrection of the dead. This fact has given rise to a misconception. Many people mistakenly believe that the Old Testament does not teach the resurrection and that the doctrine of the bodily resurrection of the dead was unknown to Old Testament Jews. This is simply not the case.

Here in the words of the angel in Daniel 12:2, the doctrine of the resurrection is beautifully presented, and it could not be more clear. Other Old Testament passages that teach the resurrection of the dead include Job 19:25–26 and Isaiah 26:19. The angel here tells Daniel that at the time when Michael arises and the time of great tribulation begins there will also be a resurrection of the dead.

We find additional details regarding this resurrection event in the New Testament. It will occur when the Lord Jesus comes for His church—the rapture. Let's look again at that profound verse from Paul's first letter to the Thessalonians: "For the Lord himself will come down from heaven, with a loud command, with the voice of the archangel and with the trumpet call of God, *and the dead in Christ will rise first*" (1 Thessalonians 4:16, emphasis added).

It's not clear whether the resurrection that Paul describes is the same resurrection that the angel describes in Daniel 12:2. The angel may refer to another resurrection that will occur at the end of the tribulation. In either event, we know that it will be a selective resurrection. Not everyone will rise from the dead at this time, as the angel tells Daniel: "Multitudes [i.e., many] who sleep in the dust of the earth will awake: some to everlasting life, others to shame and everlasting contempt."

The NIV translation blurs the meaning of the original Hebrew text of this verse. In the Hebrew, it is clear that the angel is speaking of a selective resurrection. A better translation might be, "many of those who sleep in the dust of the earth will awake; these who are risen shall receive everlasting life; those who do not arise shall receive shame and everlasting contempt."

The book of Revelation tells us that those who are resurrected at the coming of the Lord for His church take part in what's called "the first resurrection." Those who awake to shame and everlasting contempt come alive a thousand years later in what is called "the second death." Here is how the apostle John explains it in the book of Revelation:

> I saw thrones on which were seated those who had been given authority to judge. And I saw the souls of those who had been beheaded because of their testimony about Jesus and because of the word of God. They had not worshiped the beast or its image and had not received its mark on their foreheads or their hands. They came to life and reigned with Christ a thousand years. (The rest of the dead did not come to life until the thousand years were ended.) This is the first resurrection. Blessed and holy are those who share in the first resurrection. The second

death has no power over them, but they will be priests of God and of Christ and will reign with him for a thousand years. (Revelation 20:4–6)

Next, the angel tells Daniel:

"Those who are wise will shine like the brightness of the heavens, and those who lead many to righteousness, like the stars for ever and ever." (Daniel 12:3)

These are the last words of the vision. They point out the glory and honor that God has reserved for those who are faithful during this time of trial and tribulation. There will be two kinds of faithful believers in those days. First, there will be those who are wise. Literally, they are "the teachers," those who teach others the truth about God. Second, there will be those who witness by word and example, and who lead many to righteousness. Because of their faithfulness, God will honor them and they will shine like the stars in the heavens, forever and ever.

So concludes the vision the angel told to Daniel.

DECLINE AND FALL

Next, the angel gives this admonition to the prophet Daniel:

"But you, Daniel, roll up and seal the words of the scroll until the time of the end. Many will go here and there to increase knowledge." (Daniel 12:4)

Many people are puzzled by this verse. They ask, "What did the angel mean when he told Daniel to seal up the book?" Some Bible scholars have concluded that this means the book of Daniel is a cryptic book, and that it cannot be understood by mortal human beings. They claim that these prophecies are couched in such strange words and images that no one can truly understand them. The book is a riddle, they say, and will not be unveiled until we reach the last days.

But that's not what the angel means. As a matter of fact, in spite of its symbolism and imagery, the book of Daniel is actually quite simple to decipher—so simple a child could understand it. The book is made up of simple stories.

So what does it mean when the angel says to Daniel, "Roll up and seal the words of the scroll until the time of the end"? First, we must understand what scroll the angel was referring to. The angel is not talking about the book of Daniel, the book that Daniel was *writing.* The angel told Daniel to seal up the words of the scroll he was *reading.* And what scroll was Daniel reading? For the answer to that question, we must go back to Daniel 10:21—"but first I will tell you what is written in the Book of Truth." And later, in Daniel 11:2, the angel says, "Now then, I tell you the truth."

It appears that the angel had a book in front of him, and he was reading the great events of this vision from the Book of Truth. That book symbolizes God's foreknowledge of all human events. Everything that occurs in history is known to God long before it ever takes place. God's foreknowledge of history is symbolized by the book from which the angel has been reading to Daniel. At this point in the prophecy, the angel tells Daniel, in effect, "This is all I'm going to read to you. There is more future history in this scroll, but we are going to stop now, roll up the scroll, and seal these words until the time of the end. This is all that will be revealed to you now."

So the angel's words to Daniel in Daniel 12:4 had nothing to do with understanding the prophecy. In fact, the angel gave this prophecy to Daniel, and to us, so these words might be understood. God gave us the book of Daniel so we would know what will come to pass.

Many people are also mystified by the latter part of this verse: "Many will go here and there to increase knowledge." The angel is describing events that will take place until the time of the end is reached. Some people believe it is a prediction of the revolution in communication, information, and transportation in our world today, including computer technology, the Internet, radio and television, and air transportation. This may be the correct interpretation of the angel's statement.

But I rather think it is much more likely that the angel refers to an increase in knowledge of the book of Daniel. This interpretation is suggested by the fact that this statement comes immediately after the angel's counsel to "roll up and seal the words of the scroll until the time of the end." Looked at this way, this statement would mean, "Many people will go here and there throughout this vision, investigating these signs and symbols in order to increase their knowledge of God's plan for the future. The more they study it, the more their knowledge will increase."

I would hasten to add that it may not be a case of one interpretation being right and the other wrong. Sometimes two different interpretations of a given prophetic word are true. That may well be the case with this statement by the angel. Many people will study the book of Daniel and other biblical prophecy, and knowledge of prophecy will increase through the years as we approach the last days. At the same time, there will also be a rapid expansion of knowledge, information, communication, and transportation in the world at large.

It can be demonstrated that human knowledge in the secular realm is directly related to knowledge of God and His Word. When knowledge of the Bible and knowledge of God declines, we always see a decline in the secular culture as well. After the fifth century, Europe drifted into a period of ignorance, darkness, and intellectual torpor in both the Church and the secular realm. The Scriptures were not available to the common people, and when the Scriptures are no longer available, people are unable to understand very much about life. For nearly a thousand years, from the fifth century to the fifteenth century, ignorance and superstition reigned. There was very little cultural, artistic, literary, or scientific progress during all that time. Historians refer to it (appropriately enough) as the Dark Ages.

What happened in the fifteenth century to change all that? That was the dawn of the Protestant Reformation. Even before Martin Luther rediscovered the biblical principle that "the just shall live by faith," people throughout Christendom were rediscovering God's Word. At the same time, the secular world experienced a cultural and intellectual reawakening that became known as the Renaissance (meaning "the rebirth"). The Renaissance was the rebirth of knowledge and culture and intellectual curiosity. It followed immediately upon the restoration of the Scriptures as the central source of insight and wisdom in Western culture.

It's significant that the Protestant Reformers did not preach and teach very much from the prophetic passages of Scripture. They were primarily concerned with other issues. But then, around the middle of the nineteenth century, the Christian church experienced a reawakened interest in Bible prophecy. In England and America, Christians began to study the predictive passages. Major Christian conventions such as the Niagara Bible Conference were organized to proclaim prophetic truths. Bible teachers and evangelists such as John Nelson Darby, Hudson Taylor, and Cyrus Scofield preached the good news that Jesus not only lived, died, and rose again but that He is also coming again.

The nineteenth century was a time when knowledge truly increased. This vast explosion of biblical knowledge coincided with an explosion of cultural and scientific knowledge. There seems to be a strange but very real connection between our knowledge of God and our knowledge of the rest of life. And when our knowledge of God declines, as it has in the twentieth and twenty-first centuries, the culture also declines. As we move away from biblical principles, our economy becomes debased and unstable. Our culture becomes crude, violent, and given over to our baser, more animalistic impulses.

The nation that landed men on the moon in the 1960s and 1970s can no longer afford to launch space shuttles in the twenty-first century. The Internet is one of the great technological achievements of the human race, yet some experts claim that nearly half of the Internet's roughly half-billion websites are devoted to pornography. Our television screens, movies, books, films, and magazines are awash in moral sewage. And our nation spends a trillion dollars more per year than it takes in—with no plan to ever pay down the mounting debt. This is what happens to a nation that rejects knowledge of God. This is what happens to a nation that removes God's Word from classrooms and courtrooms and legislatures and the public square.

There are hidden secrets of life that God has revealed to us in His Word. When we reject that knowledge, we doom our society to a decline and fall that's every bit as terrible as the fall of Rome.

THE MAN CLOTHED IN LINEN

In the next few verses, the man clothed in linen we met in Daniel 10 makes a final appearance. As we've already established, this man is a preincarnate, Old Testament appearance of the Lord Jesus. There is a brief and fascinating dialogue between Daniel and the Lord:

> Then I, Daniel, looked, and there before me stood two others, one on this bank of the river and one on the opposite bank. One of them said to the man clothed in linen, who was above the waters of the river, "How long will it be before these astonishing things are fulfilled?"
>
> The man clothed in linen, who was above the waters of the river, lifted his right hand and his left hand toward heaven, and I heard him swear by him who lives forever, saying, "It will be for a time, times and half a time. When the power of the holy people has been finally broken, all these things will be completed." (Daniel 12:5–7)

This vision began when Daniel saw the man clothed in linen, with a bright countenance, standing by the river. Now at the end of the vision, Daniel again sees this man, accompanied by two angels.

The angels stand on either bank of the river, and the man clothed in linen seems to stand upon or hover over the river waters. Daniel asks, "How long will it be before these astonishing things are fulfilled?"

The question is understandable. Daniel has just seen a vision of the time of indescribable trouble for his people. Daniel finds this vision painful and disturbing, and he identifies and empathizes with his suffering people. So he asks when these events will come to pass.

And the Lord Jesus, the man clothed in linen, raises His right hand to indicate the solemnity and trustworthiness of His words, much as a witness in a courtroom raises his right hand and swears to tell the truth, the whole truth, and nothing but the truth. This gesture reminds us of when Jesus, during His earthly ministry, would underscore His words by saying, "Truly, truly I say to you." To Daniel, He guarantees His word with an upraised hand and says, "It will be for a time, times and half a time. When the power of the holy people has been finally broken, all these things will be completed." As we've already seen in our study of Daniel, the phrase "a time, times and half a time" refers to three and a half years (a "time" is a year).

Then He says, "When the power of the holy people has been finally broken, all these things will be completed." This is an important sign. The Lord is telling us that Israel is going to have a magnified influence in world affairs in the future. The Jewish people will have remarkable power—a power and influence so impressive that the Western nations, the confederacy of the West, will make a covenant with Israel. As a result of this covenant, the nation of Israel will have a dominant role in world affairs.

But at the end of the three and a half years ("a time, times and half a time"), the power of Israel will be shattered and broken. The nation will be defeated and crushed as never before. By the close of Daniel's seventieth week, the power of Israel will be broken. The people of Israel will be cast utterly upon the grace of their loving God.

Daniel wants to know more. He wants to understand more fully what the future holds for his people. So Daniel interrupts the man clothed in linen:

> I heard, but I did not understand. So I asked, "My lord, what will the outcome of all this be?"
>
> He replied, "Go your way, Daniel, because the words are rolled up and sealed until the time of the end. Many will be purified, made spotless and refined, but the wicked will continue to be wicked. None of the wicked will understand, but those who are wise will understand." (Daniel 12:8–10)

Daniel wants to know what it means when the man clothed in linen says, "When the power of the holy people has been finally broken, all these things will be completed." This sounds ominous and mysterious. Why must the power of the Jewish people be broken? What does it all mean?

But the man clothed in linen has revealed all that can be revealed. "Go your way, Daniel," the Lord tells him, in effect. "There will be no more revelations to you from the Book of Truth. The book is closed. I can tell you nothing more." Yet there is value in studying all that has been revealed. The Lord adds, "Many will be purified, made spotless and refined, but the wicked will continue to be wicked. None of the wicked will understand, but those who are wise will understand."

Here the man clothed in linen—the Lord Jesus—refers to the book of Daniel, in which all that has been revealed to Daniel will be written and preserved. Many shall read it, study it, and search it through—and the result of all of that study will be threefold:

First, people will interact with the book of Daniel. Those who are wise will purify themselves by reading the cleansing Word of God, which is always a powerful and effective cleansing agent.

Second, people with act upon the Word as they read it, and they will be made spotless and refined. They will become righteous, godly, moral people.

Third, some people will read the book of Daniel, but they will not understand it—and they will continue to do wickedly. The Lord says, "The wicked will continue to be wicked. None of the wicked will understand." He does not say that they are wicked because they do wickedly. He says that they will do wickedly because they are wicked. You may think this is hairsplitting, but it is actually a profound distinction.

A wicked person is someone who will not listen to God and who thinks he is completely self-sufficient. A person who says, "I can get along without God" is a wicked person by definition. From this defiant and self-sufficient attitude come all of their wicked acts. Their deeds become wicked because their thoughts are already wicked. This is the result, the Lord tells Daniel, of reading the book with a wicked heart and without true wisdom and understanding.

THE LAST WORD

The man clothed in linen resumes what He was telling Daniel before his interruption:

> "From the time that the daily sacrifice is abolished and the abomination that causes desolation is set up, there will be 1,290 days. Blessed is the one who waits for and reaches the end of the 1,335 days.
>
> "As for you, go your way till the end. You will rest, and then at the end of the days you will rise to receive your allotted inheritance." (Daniel 12:11–13)

The Lord lays out a timeline for the great tribulation. He says that the starting point is the final desecration of the temple, when the false prophet sets up the abomination of desolation. This takes place in the middle of the seven-year period that we call Daniel's seventieth week. From the time of the abomination of desolation, there shall be twelve hundred and ninety days. Three and a half years equals twelve hundred and sixty days, so the man clothed in linen has added an additional thirty days beyond the three and a half year period.

What is the meaning of that additional thirty days? The Lord does not say. Perhaps it involves a time of cleansing the land after the return of the Lord. But Scripture is silent on that point.

Then the man clothed in linen says, "Blessed is the one who waits for and reaches the end of the 1,335 days." That would be an *additional* forty-five days. Thirty days plus forty-five days equals an additional seventy-five days beyond the three and a half years of the great tribulation.

What is the meaning of the additional seventy-five days? Again, the Lord does not say. Perhaps this additional period of time introduces the day of the millennium, the golden age of planet Earth, when God sets up His final kingdom and righteousness shall cover the earth as the waters cover the sea. It's an inviting thought, but once again, Scripture is silent on that point.

Finally, the man clothed in linen tells Daniel, "As for you, go your way till the end. You will rest . . ." This means, of course, that Daniel will die. But the man goes on to tell Daniel, "At the end of the days you will rise to receive your allotted inheritance." The Lord promises Daniel that he will take part in the resurrection. He will not be forgotten. God will raise him up, and he will stand in his place at the end of the days.

Centuries have come and gone since these words were written. To us in the twenty-first century, Daniel is a dim figure from ancient history. But God's Word is certain. His promises are trustworthy. We can look forward with confidence to meeting Daniel someday and learning of the work God will give him to do in the ages and ages to come. Just as Peter, James, and John saw Moses and Elijah on the Mount of Transfiguration with the Lord Jesus (see Matthew 17, Mark 9, and Luke 9), we have been given a glimpse of Daniel's resurrection and return. Those who have placed their trust in God have no need to fear death, because eternal life awaits, and God has work for us to do in His new and glorious kingdom.

That is the final word, the close of the book of Daniel. But there is still a question that each of us must answer: What is our response to this book? What is our reply to this prophecy? Do we feel frightened by it? Judged by it? Depressed by it? Indifferent to it?

Or do the prophecies of Daniel drive us to purify our motives and face spiritual reality? Does this book move us to recommit our hearts to God? Do we feel encouraged and motivated to tell others about the good news of Jesus Christ? Do we feel thrilled and cheered at the thought of the Lord's returning?

The book of Daniel is like litmus paper. The way you respond to this book tells you the true state of your heart. It tells you whether you are faithful or faithless, wise or wicked, ready or reluctant. It tells you whether your eyes are open—or your heart is closed.

You cannot read the book of Daniel and remain neutral. It demands that you choose sides. Either you will choose to be on the Lord's side and be ready when He comes—or you choose the delusion and destruction that is coming on the world. How do you answer the book of Daniel?

If you have never surrendered your life to Jesus Christ, if you have never taken the step of choosing to be on the Lord's side, now and for all eternity, you can do so right now. You can pray a prayer of commitment at this very moment, before you turn the page—and the moment you pray that prayer in all sincerity, you will move from death to life, from destruction to resurrection and an eternity with God. If that is the decision of your heart right now, then please pray these words with me:

Heavenly Father,

Thank You for loving me and sending Your Son Jesus to pay the price for my sins. I confess that I have sinned many times, but I choose to turn away from my sins and to live for You. I invite Jesus to come into my life, forgive my sins, and take control as my Lord and Savior. Please seal this decision I have made and help me to live every day of my life for You. Thank You for hearing my prayer.

In the name of Jesus, Amen.

May the great prophetic message of the book of Daniel encourage you and inspire you in the coming days. May it increase your wisdom and understanding as you grow in your relationship with Christ. And may it embolden your faith as you live courageously in the coming days.

The words of this prophecy will be fulfilled exactly as written. That is our confidence. That is our hope. Come, Lord Jesus.

NOTES

Chapter 2: When Dreams Come True

1. Walter E. Wegner, *The Book of Daniel and the Dead Sea Scrolls*, originally presented as a paper in a University of Wisconsin seminar series on the Dead Sea Scrolls, date unknown, page 7, http://www.wlsessays.net /files/WegnerDaniel.pdf.

2. Richard Chenevix Trench, D.D., *Synonyms of the New Testament* (London, 1880; digitized by Ted Hildebrandt, Gordon College, Wenham, Massachusetts, 2006), 211, http://faculty.gordon.edu/hu/bi/Ted_Hildebrandt /New_Testament_Greek/Text/Trench-Synonyms.pdf.

Chapter 3: The Last Act

1. Nicene and Post-Nicene Fathers: Series II, Vol. VI, The Letters of St. Jerome, Letter 127, paragraph 12, http://en.wikisource.org/wiki /Nicene_and_Post-Nicene_Fathers:_Series_II/Volume_VI/The_Letters _of_St._Jerome/Letter_127.

2. Richard Langworth, *Churchill by Himself: The Definitive Collection of Quotations* (New York: Perseus / Public Affairs, 2008), 573.

3. Loren Collins, "The Truth About Tytler," LorenCollins.net, January 25, 2009, http://www.lorencollins.net/tytler.html.

Chapter 4: The World Menagerie

1. Søren Kierkegaard, Howard V. Hong, "Either/Or, A Fragment of Life," *The Essential Kierkegaard* (Princeton, NJ: Princeton University Press, 2000), 41.

2. Sir Robert Anderson, *The Coming Prince: The Marvelous Prophecy of Daniel's Seventy Weeks concerning the Antichrist* (New York: Cosimo, 2007), 277.

Chapter 5: The Coming Caesar

1. Winston Churchill, speech, October 11, 1950, quoted by Kenneth W. Thompson, *Winston Churchill's World View: Statesmanship and Power* (Baton Rouge, LA: LSU Press, 1983), 284.

2. Edward Teller with Allen Brown, *The Legacy of Hiroshima* (Westport, CT: Greenwood Press, 1975), 209.

3. Strobe Talbott, "The Birth of the Global Nation," *Time*, July 20, 1992, http://www.worldbeyondborders.org/globalnation.htm.

4. Walter Cronkite, "National Sovereignty and the Future of the World," address upon receiving the Norman Cousins Global Governance Award, October 19, 1999, UN Delegates Dining Room, New York City, http://www.renewamerica.com/article/050525.

5. Robert Muller, "Ideas & Dreams for a Better World," August 1999, RobertMuller.org, http://robertmuller.org/ideas/.

6. Dwight Kinman, *The World's Last Dictator* (New Kinsington, PA: Whitaker House, 1993), 81; see also Thomas Ivan Dahlheimer, "Proposed Occupy Wall Street Global Initiative," Towahkon.org, January 25, 2012, http://www.towahkon.org/GlobalInitiative.html.

7. Michael J. Panzner, *When Giants Fall: An Economic Roadmap for the End of the American Era* (Hoboken, NJ: Wiley & Sons, 2009), 6–7.

8. David M. Walker, *Comeback America: Turning the Country Around and Restoring Fiscal Responsibility* (New York: Random House, 2009), 36–37.

9. Niall Ferguson, "Complexity and Collapse: Empires on the Edge of Chaos," Foreign Affairs, Published by the Council on Foreign Relations, March/April 2010, http://www.foreignaffairs.com/articles/65987/niall-ferguson/complexity-and-collapse.

10. Staff report, "Did Psychic Jeane Dixon Predict JFK's Assassination?" StraightDope.com, February 2, 2000, http://www.straightdope.com/columns/read/1736/did-psychic-jeane-dixon-predict-jfks-assassination.

11. Ruth Montgomery, *A Gift of Prophecy* (New York: Bantam, 1966), 181.

Chapter 6: The Great Propagandist

1. *The Works of Flavius Josephus*, William Whiston, translator (1737), "Antiquities of the Jews," Book XI, chapter 8, paragraph 5, http://sacred-texts.com/jud/josephus/ant-11.htm.

Chapter 7: God's Countdown

1. Hippolytus of Rome, "Treatise on Christ and Antichrist," EarlyChristian Writings.com, http://www.earlychristianwritings.com/text/hippolytus-christ.html.

Chapter 8: The Other Side of Prayer

1. Dr. Helen Roseveare, "The Hot Water Bottle," TruthOrFiction.com, http://www.truthorfiction.com/rumors/h/hotwaterbottle.htm.

NOTE TO THE READER

The publisher invites you to share your response to the message of this book by writing Discovery House Publishers, P.O. Box 3566, Grand Rapids, MI 49501, U.S.A. For information about other Discovery House books, music, videos, or DVDs, contact us at the same address or call 1-800-653-8333. Find us on the Internet at www.dhp.org or send e-mail to books@dhp.org.